Catering For A Dinner Party At Home

Where do you begin, what is in season and how do I compliment each course. Soup, hot or cold starter, fish poached or fried, do I need lamb, beef, pork or poultry and to finish is it going to be a hot or cold sweet? These are the questions that we all make and cannot decide, well help is at hand. I have produced 12 menus, one for each month which will enchant your guest's and give you total satisfaction.

Let me tell you a little bit about myself so you get an insight to where I was trained and what experience I have gained during my career. I was trained at Westminster Hotel School in London where I did a two-year Chef's course passing out with a credit for theory and a distinction for my practical work. During my time at college I spent time working at the fish, meat and vegetable markets to know how to buy good quality produce and to know where it came from I did this either early mornings or after college, which gave me an idea of all the good things to look for when purchasing food.

During the holidays I worked in prestigious hotels such as the Dorchester in London, Saunton Sands Hotel Devon, University College Hospital London and was lucky enough to be asked to work on the Coronation Ball held at the Royal Albert Hall in London so before I was let loose on the public I had some experience under my belt.

As a good person I did my National Service in the Army Catering Corps where I did my basic training on the parade ground square-bashing but then they let me loose in the kitchen this I enjoyed and with my experience I was posted to Nottingham as chef for Major-General F.D.Moore where I had to do diner parties and buffets for him while he was entertaining important people in the Services.

After National Service I worked for a while in Nottingham as a chef at the Black Boy Hotel, but wanted more so moved to Paris and worked under a Mr Olivier at the restaurant Velfour. During this time I learned a lot about cuisine and also had to master French, this was helped by a family I stayed with in Paris who were very good to me.

After my stint in Paris I moved to London as a chef at the Carlton Tower Hotel under Louis Cippola who really wanted the best out of his brigade. Here I was lucky to go round all the different parts of the kitchen and relieve the chef's when they had a day off or to cover for holidays which gave me a lot of experience. During my time there I was asked to look after Prince Ranier and Grace Kelly which was an honour and after some time they asked me if I would work for them in Monaco this I turned down as I wanted to run my own kitchen.

I was asked by a Mrs Fox w... would like to head a new p... de L'Aperatif which sounde... required, I said yes and ope... the best and after only six months rave reviews were made a... food we were serving. After a few years it was voted one of the best restaurants in the Midlands so after this success I looked for pastures new.

Industrial catering was my next venture where I joined a firm called Midland Catering which operated works canteens and Directors dining rooms rather different from hotels. I was based at their flagship and head office in Nottingham, Meridian on Hayden Road here I had about 2000 people to feed plus a Directors and Staff Dining rooms to look after, we had our own bakery unit where we produced cakes and pastries daily and I would order about 3 ton of potatoes a week.

After only 18 months I was offered the position of area supervisor for the Company where I looked after twelve units in the Nottingham area where I had to control hygiene, cost and quality control, which was a challenge as many of the staff had not got a lot of experience so had to set about showing them how to do some of the dishes that they could produce without a lot of fuss which proved a great success.

I looked carefully at this section of the market and decided to set up my own Company offering my services to Industry. Here I started very slowly but after a while firms realised that I was giving value for money and after several years of hard work and training I was operating over 70 units for different clients and had my own training school where people were trained for positions in the Company.

There was a lot of hard work here and I was not cooking but managing so the Company was sold and I reverted to working for someone else I joined British Gypsum as catering manager where I could do more cooking, this I enjoyed·very much as I could create my own dishes and while at Gypsum I entered a number of culinary competitions winning gold, silver and bronze medals and having my work accepted on the Table of Honour.

I am a member of the Association Culinaire Francaise where The Gold Medal Maitrise Escoffier was awarded to me. I am a member of the Craft Guild of Chefs where I am a master craftsman, and a member of the Midland Association of Chefs.

Happy cooking

John Thorp

John Thorp

Menu for January

Crab and Avocado Rondelles
served with a Sherry, Honey & Basil Vinaigrette

***

Pasta with Bacon, Mushrooms and Tomatoes

***

Poached Fillet Steak in Red Wine Sauce
Macaire Potatoes
Stuffed Braised Cabbage
Turnips Berrichone

***

Apple Creme Brulle

Menu for February

Celery and Stilton Soup

***

Provencale Tart Topped with Cod
served with a Red Pepper Sauce

***

Pork with Stuffed Apples
Potato Au Gratin
Limed Glazed Parsnips
Courgettes Provencale

***

Individual Bread and Butter Pudding

Menu for May

Fresh Asparagus
served with a Creamy Hollandaise Sauce

***

Escallop of Wild Salmon

***

Poussin with Grapes
Potato and Mushroom Medley
Stuffed Baby Courgettes
served on a bed of Rice
Buttered Mange Tout

***

Zabaglione with Langues De Chat Biscuits

Menu for June

Baked Goats Cheese and Vegetable Pyramids
with Lemon and Walnut Vinaigrette
***
Chicken, Spinach and Smoked Bacon Roulade
with Cumberland Sauce
***
Lamb Fillets in Filo Pastry
served with Tomato, Mint and Courgette Salsa
Boulangere Potatoes
Fresh Green Beans wrapped in Bacon
Golden Top Cauliflower
***
Grand Marnier and Apricot Alaska

All menus serve six people

Menu for March

Avocado with Prawns and Pink Grapefruit

***

Cauliflower and Bacon Ramekin

***

Duck Casserole
with Apricots, Mint and Pine Nuts
Grilled Lemony Potatoes
Red Cabbage Asascienne
Carrots Glace

***

Brandied Fruity Pancakes

Menu for April

Half a Melon with Orange and Ginger

***

Honey Glazed Tuna on a Mixed Salad

***

Roast Rack of Lamb
Garlic and Potato Patties
Glazed Shallots
Braised Spring Cabbage Balls

***

Chocolate Mousse

Menu for July

Gazpacho

***

Scampi Harlequin with Rice

***

Beef Encroute
Normande Potatoes
Celery Almondine
Oriental Salad

***

Raspberries in a Wine Jelly

Menu for August

Arancini Di Riso

***

Pasta Trampanese

***

Farsumagru
Caponata

***

Sicilian Peaches

All menus serve six people

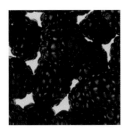

Menu for September

Smoked Salmon Mousse
***
Tomato Jelly
with Smoked Ham served with a
Horseradish Vinaigrette
***
Roast Grouse with Blackberry Sauce
Chilli Roast Potatoes
Filo Boats filled with Leek Puree
Broccoli Polonaise
***
Caramelised Rice Pudding and Oranges with a
Ginger Caramelised sauce

Menu for October

Twiced Baked Cheese and Bacon Souffle
with a Roasted Red Pepper Sauce
***
Warm Salad of Red Mullet
served with a Lemon Balm Dressing
***
Pheasant Breasts
with Grapes and Mushrooms
Marquise Potatoes
Braised Fennel Au Gratin
Vichy Carrots
***
Poached Pears
served with a Vanilla Cream Sauce

Menu for November

Stilton, Watercress and Walnut Terrine
with Sherry and Tomato Cream
***
Rubane of Halibut with Pink Grapefruit
with White Wine Sauce
***
Stuffed Loin of Pork
with a Sage and Garlic Crust
and a Maderia Sauce
Stir Fried Sprouts with Pinenuts
Parsnip Gratin with Horseradish Cream
Fondante Potatoes
***
Armagnac Parfait in a Brandy Snap Basket
with Oranges and Earl Grey Syrup

Menu for December

Red Pepper and Courgette Mousse
with a Lime and Parsley Hollandaise

***
Melon Cocktail with Prawns

***
Tomato and Herb Crusted fillet of Beef
Spiced Creamy Potatoes
Fantail Lemon Garlic Potatoes
Buttered Leeks and Tarragon
Buttered Sprouts with Almonds

***
Chocolate Meringue Log

All menus serve six people

Avocado with Prawns
Turn to page: 12

Melon & Orange
Turn to page: 16

Asparagus with Hollandaise Sauce
Turn to page: 21

Red Pepper & Courgette Mousse
Turn to page: 56

Vegetable Pyramids
Turn to page: 26

Twice Baked Souffle
Turn to page: 46

Crab and Avocado Rondelles
Turn to page: 1

Smoked Salmon Mousse
Turn to page: 41

Escallop of Wild Salmon
Turn to page: 22

Pasta with Bacon, Mushrooms and Tomatoes
Turn to page: 2

Scampi Harlequin with Rice
Turn to page: 32

Pasta Trampanese
Turn to page: 37

Provencale Tart Topped with Cod
Turn to page: 7

Fresh Green Beans wrapped in Bacon
Turn to page: 29

Arancini Di Roso
Turn to page: 36

Tomato Jelly with Smoked Ham
Turn to page: 42

Tomato & Herb Crusted Fillet of Beef
Turn to page: 58

Beef En Croute
Turn to page: 33

Poussin with Grapes
Turn to page: 23

Pork with Stuffed Apples
Turn to page: 8

Roast Rack of Lamb
Turn to page: 18

Lamb Fillets in Filo Pastry
Turn to page: 28

Duck with Apricots & Mint
Turn to page: 13

Farsumagru
Turn to page: 38

*Armagnac Parfait in a Brandy Snap Basket
with Oranges and Earl Grey Syrup*
Turn to page: 55

Raspberries in a Wine Jelly
Turn to page:35

Brandied Fruity Pancakes
Turn to page: 15

Grand Marnier & Apricot Alaska
Turn to page: 30

Chocolate Mousse
Turn to page: 20

*Caramelised Rice Pudding and Oranges
with a Ginger Caramelised Sauce*
Turn to page: 45

Chocolate Meringue Log
Turn to page: 61

Raspberries in a Wine Jelly
Turn to page: 35

The days are cold and maybe there is snow on the ground. The nights have drawn in, it is also just after Christmas fare when poultry has been eaten with that stodgy Christmas Pudding and Mince Pies so let us change all that for a nice refreshing meal.

With this menu you can prepare the starter and sweet in advance, which will leave you plenty of time to get relaxed for a nice evening with your guests especially after the hectic Christmas entertaining.

CRAB AND AVOCADO RONDELLES
SERVED WITH A SHERRY, HONEY & BASIL VINAIGRETTE

(Prep time: 20 minutes)

8 oz / 250g crabmeat

2 avocados

Juice of one lemon

4 tomatoes skinned, pips removed and diced

Chopped dill

Place a slightly oiled stainless steel mould on a plate place some of the tomatoes in the bottom.

Peel the avocado and remove the stone, place cut side down then slice, do this to all the avocados put in a basin, sprinkle with lemon juice to stop them discolouring. Place some slices of avocado on top of the tomatoes, press down lightly. Carefully mix the crabmeat with the dill and place on top of the avocados press down lightly.

Finish with another layer of avocado, top with the remaining tomato press down to make firm. Place in the refrigerator till about an hour before you are ready to serve. When ready carefully remove the stainless ring by twisting a little first then removing altogether. Drizzle the sauce around the plate and serve with some buttered brown bread.

Sauce

Prep time: 5 minutes

2 tablespoons of clear honey

4 tablespoons of sherry vinegar

1 tablespoon of oil

8 leaves basil

Combine all the ingredients together except the basil.

When mixed, taste to get an idea of the bitterness of the vinegar and sweetness of the honey and adapt to you're requirement. Finely shred the basil and add to the mixture.

Top Tip

This dish can be made well in advance

1

PASTA WITH BACON, MUSHROOMS AND TOMATOES

Prep time: 10 minutes

Cooking Time: 20 minutes

8 oz / 225g Pasta Shells

4 oz / 100g streaky bacon sliced

6 oz / 175g button mushrooms

3 tablespoons oil

Chopped parsley & basil

1 tin of chopped tomatoes

Cook pasta in boiling salted water for 10 to 12 minutes when cooked refresh under cold water, drain well. Heat oil in a wok add the bacon and cook for approximately 2 to 3 minutes, add the washed button mushrooms cook for a further 3 minutes till cooked.

Add the pasta and mix thoroughly stir in the tomatoes and herbs heat through, season and serve sprinkling a little chopped parsley on top for presentation.

Top Tip

If you cook the pasta well in advance which I recommend, to make it easy for you on the day, leave in cold water or else it will stick together

POACHED FILLET STEAK IN RED WINE SAUCE

Prep time: 45 minutes

Cooking Time: 20-30 minutes

6 x 7 oz / 200g fillet steaks

(order from your butcher ask him to tie them round the middle)

1 bottle red wine

1 small leek

1 onion

1 carrot

1 stick of celery

$\frac{1}{2}$ oz / 15g chopped parsley

$\frac{1}{2}$ clove of garlic

4 oz / 100g butter

2 tbsp of double cream

Wash peel and chop roughly all the vegetables put into a saucepan cover with water and bring to the boil allow to simmer for about 30 minutes.

Add red wine and bring to the boil then allow them to simmer for 5 minutes. Seal the steaks in a hot frying pan, add to the liquor, bring to the boil and simmer for about 7 minutes for a medium steak, 4 minutes for rare and about 10 minutes for a well-done steak.

Remove when cooked and keep warm for a while. Meanwhile strain the liquor and reduce rapidly till the sauce begins to thicken, take off the stove add butter so it becomes thick and a nice glaze finally add cream, taste the sauce season as required.

Remove the string from the steaks and put on a hot plate and pour the sauce over. Sprinkle with the chopped parsley.

MACAIRE POTATOES

Prep time: 35 minutes
Cooking Time: 10 minutes

4 Medium Jacket Potatoes

Nutmeg

Seasoning

Chopped Parsley

Flour

Cook jacket potatoes in the oven when cooked cut in half, length ways, remove the pulp into a basin and mash well, season with salt, pepper and nutmeg.

Add butter, chopped parsley and mix well together. Form into a medallion shape, sprinkle with flour, mark criss-cross with a knife on the top, saute them in clarified butter and oil, best side down first to a golden brown, turn over with a palette knife, serve on a dish sprinkle with chopped parsley.

Top Tip

These can be made in advance so they only need to be fried when required

STUFFED BRAISED CABBAGE

Prep time: 20 minutes
Cooking Time: 15 minutes

Take one Savoy cabbage and remove the outer leaves, wash well in cold water then remove the thick stalk through the middle without cutting the leaf in two. Blanch these in boiling salted water with a touch of sugar to retain the green colour, refresh in running cold water. The remaining cabbage cut in quarters wash well, then cook in boiling salted water till almost cooked, strain in a colander, season and chop up to remove the water content.

Arrange the outer leaves on a chopping board, scoop some of your cabbage in the centre of the leaves, lap over each side roll up to form a parcel, place in a buttered dish when all are in the dish cover with a buttered paper. Put a little stock in the bottom and braise in the oven for approximately 15 minutes. You could add a little cooked carrot to your mixture to give extra colour.

Top Tip
Make into parcels in the morning and leave in dish ready to cook

TURNIPS BERRICHONNE

Prep time: 10 minutes
Cooking Time: 35 minutes

2 lb / 900g turnips

4 oz / 100g streaky bacon

4 oz / 100g chopped onions

Chopped parsley

$1/_2$ pint chicken stock

Peel the turnips with a knife turn barrel shape, place in cold water. Cut the bacon into strips, fry without colour in a pan, add your onions and gently fry together. Place turnips in a casserole dish add onions and bacon, barely cover with the stock, cover with buttered paper and cook gently in the oven. When cooked place in a serving dish, reduce the liquor by half, and mask over the turnips, finish with chopped parsley.

Top Tip
Prepare the turnips in the morning and leave in cold water

4

APPLE CREME BRULLE

Prep time: 25 minutes

Cooking time: 40 minutes

1 lb / 450g dessert apples peeled and chopped

2 tbsp lemon juice

1 oz / 25g sultanas

1 pt double cream

5 egg yolks

1 egg

4 oz / 100g castor sugar

4 tbsp demerara sugar

3 tbsp rum or brandy

Put the apples, lemon juice and a little water in a pan. Cover with a lid and simmer gently for about 10 minutes or until the apples have pulped, stir in the sultanas and leave to cool. Beat the egg and egg yolks with the castor sugar in a bowl till quite white in colour, bring the cream to the boil in a saucepan then slowly add to the mixture beating all the time to prevent it from curdling. When thoroughly mixed add the rum or brandy and strain through a fine conical strainer.

Put some of the apple mixture in the bottom of the ramekin top up with your egg and cream mixture, place in a tray, cover half way up with warm water and cook in an oven 170C/325F/Gas mark 3 for 40-45 minutes until just set, remove and allow to cool. Top each ramekin with the Demerara sugar and place under a really hot grill for 3-4 minutes until the sugar has melted and a nice golden brown. Leave to cool, and chill for one hour before serving.

Serve this sweet on a plate with a doily; this will help the ramekin to stay firm on the plate. This is a very light sweet very delicate and will leave your guests on a high especially after the main course, which is quite substantial.

Top Tip

This can be made well in advance

FEBRUARY

It is still cold and the party season for Christmas and New Year is over. You have served your first meal for January and now is the time to be a bit more adventurous.

With this menu you can make the soup and salmon mousse in advance, and prepare the pudding ready for the oven.

This leaves you with the pork and vegetables to cook fresh but remember to put the bread and butter puddings in the oven after the pork is removed, as they will take 35 minutes to cook.

CELERY & STILTON SOUP

Prep time: 8 minutes

Cooking time: 30 minutes

2 heads of celery cleaned and finely chopped

2 onions chopped

1 small potato, diced

1 pt milk

1 pt vegetable stock

1 bay leaf

8 oz / 225g Stilton crumbled

1/2 baguette Thinly sliced

Freshly snipped chives for garnish

1oz / 25g butter

Melt the butter in a large pan add the celery and onions. Cook together for approximately 3 minutes stirring constantly, cover with a lid and simmer for 5 minutes till the vegetables are soft.

Add the potato, milk, stock and bay leaf, cover with a lid bring to the boil and simmer for 30 minutes.

Remove the bay leaf.

Add 6 oz of the Stilton and blend in a mixer till smooth. Pass through a conical strainer, return to pan and season to taste.

You can make this soup richer if you stir in cream before serving. Sprinkle the rest of the Stilton on the sliced baguettes and toast under the grill.

Put the soup in bowls add the Stilton toasts sprinkle with chives.

PROVENCALE TART TOPPED WITH COD
SERVED WITH A RED PEPPER SAUCE

Prep time: 30 minutes

Cooking time: 20 minutes

PASTRY

7 oz / 200g Plain flour

3½ oz / 100g butter

Mixed herbs

2-3 tbsp cold water

FOR THE FILLING

1lb / 450g cod fillet

2 red peppers

6 oz / 175g Goats cheese or grated strong cheddar

2 firm tomatoes skinned and sliced

2 oz / 50g mushrooms sliced

1 oz / 25g butter

4floz double cream

Put the flour and a pinch of salt into a food processor, add the butter, whiz till you get fine crumbs.

Add the herbs and with the motor running gradually add the water till the pastry comes together. Remove, wrap in cling film, chill for 30 minutes.

Roll out the pastry, line 6 large tartlet moulds, and prick the base with a fork, chill for 15 minutes.

Preheat oven to gas mark 6/200C/400F. Line the moulds with greaseproof paper and fill with dried beans, bake for 15 minutes, remove dried beans and paper and cook for a further 10 minutes till pastry is golden and cooked.

FILLING
Put the peppers in a hot oven till the skins are blackened, remove into a plastic bag and leave to cool then remove the skins and seeds. Cut into strips.

Melt the butter in a pan add the onions and sweat for 4 minutes making sure they do not colour, cut up the cod into cubes add to the onions, stir together for only one minute, season add the cream to bind the cod.

Divide the mushrooms on the bottom of the pastry cases, add a slice of tomato on top, season, then top with the cod filling, place on top strips of red peppers, and finish with either the Goats cheese or cheddar as desired. Cook for a further 10 minutes or until beginning to brown.

SAUCE
Melt 1 oz/25g butter in a pan add 1 oz/25g plain flour mix together to make a roux, add some milk slowly and some dry white wine to make a sauce add some chopped red peppers left over from the tarts with any juice you may have left, season for taste.

Put some sauce on a plate add a tart and serve immediately.

Top Tip

You can make your tart bases in advance and freeze until required

7

PORK WITH STUFFED APPLES

Prep time: 10 minutes

Cooking time: 2 hours

3 lb / 1350g leg of pork
(boned and rolled)

6 or 8 red apples

1 finely chopped onion

4 oz / 100g fresh white breadcrumbs

2 oz / 50g sultanas

1 oz / 25g dried sage

3 oz / 75g butter

2 tbls clear honey

$^1/_2$ pint cider

1 tbsp gravy mix

Preheat the oven to 220C/425F/Gas 7.

Put the pork in a roasting tray spread with honey, drizzle over with a little oil, sprinkle with salt, put a little water on the bottom of the roasting tray to cover the base, roast for 30 minutes then reduce heat 190C/375F/Gas 5, continue to cook for a further 1 hour 30 minutes basting every 30 minutes.

To make the stuffed apples melt butter in a pan add the onions, sweat for 5 minutes. Stir in the breadcrumbs, sultanas and sage, cook together for a minute.

Cut the top of the apples zigzag and remove, cut out the core. Chop the top of the apple into dice and mix with the stuffing, add the mixture to the apples.

Half an hour before the pork is cooked, add apples to the roasting tray and carry on cooking so the flavour of the pork is passed on to the apples.

When pork is cooked remove with the apples and keep warm. To make the gravy remove the fat from the roasting pan add the cider, bring to the boil stirring all the time, dilute the gravy mix then add to your gravy cook out for a few minutes until smooth and semi thick, strain and put into sauce boats.

Remove the crackling from the pork, cut up into slices and place on a flat or dish serve with the apples and garnish with watercress.

POTATO AU GRATIN

Prep time: 10 minutes
Cooking time: 1 1/2 hours

2 lb / 900g potatoes peeled and sliced thinly

2 large onions sliced thinly

6 oz / 175g grated strong cheddar cheese

8 fl oz milk

8 fl oz double cream

2 oz / 50g butter

1 oz / 25g plain flour

Chopped parsley

Seasoning

Make a roux with the flour and 1 oz of butter add the milk and cream to make a thin white sauce. Preheat the oven to 180C/350F/Gas 4.

Butter a large ovenproof dish layer with potatoes, onions, parsley and cheese, season each layer finish with potatoes neatly overlapping on top.

Add the sauce, sprinkle with cheese on top, place in oven, cook for about 1hour 30 minutes until the potatoes are tender when pierced with a skewer.

LIME GLAZED PARSNIPS

Prep time: 6 minutes
Cooking time: 1 hour

1 lb / 450g parsnips peeled

1 lime
(with the zest taken off and finely shred into strips, segment the lime)

1 finely chopped onion

2 oz / 50g butter

Chopped parsley

Seasoning

Cut parsnips into chunks and wash. Preheat oven to 180C/350F/Gas 5 put the butter into dish and melt, add parsnips season and place in the oven for about 45 minutes.

Meanwhile put the shredded zest into a pan with water and blanche well, refresh under cold water then drain. Remove the parsnips from the oven add the onions and lime segments mix well, cook for a further 15 minutes.

Remove from oven when cooked place in a serving dish sprinkle with the zest and chopped parsley.

COURGETTES PROVENCALE

Prep time: 6 minutes

Cooking time: 30 minutes

1 lb / 450g courgettes sliced

3 small cloves of garlic

1 tin chopped tomatoes

$^1/_2$ tsp chopped fresh oregano

3 tbsp oil

2 sliced onions

Heat the oil in a pan, add the onions and crushed garlic, sweat together with a lid on for about 5 minutes.

Add the courgettes and mix well together. Season and mix in the tomatoes and oregano cover with a lid and cook for about 20 minutes or until the courgettes are tender.

Serve in appropriate dish.

To make this dish interesting you could roast some flaked almonds about 3 oz and sprinkle them on top when serving.

INDIVIDUAL BREAD & BUTTER PUDDINGS

Prep time: 8 minutes

Cooking time: 40-45 minutes

4 slices of white bread
(which has been buttered)

4 oz / 100g mixed dried fruit

2 oz / 50g butter

1 pt milk

4 eggs

4 oz / 100g castor sugar

Vanilla essence

Nutmeg

For this dish you will need 6 empty 200g baked bean tins.

Wash your tin well and dry butter the inside and coat with sugar, this enables you to remove the pudding when cooked.

With a round cutter the size of the tin cut 6 rounds of bread.

Sprinkle the mixed fruit in the bottom of the tins, add the buttered rounds of bread. In a pan put $1/2$ pint milk with the sugar and essence bring to the boil and remove, beat the eggs with the other $1/2$ pint of milk, mix with the boiled milk, strain through a conical strainer. Pour over the tins to half way, allow to stand for 15 minutes, pour in the remaining milk to the rim, sprinkle with nutmeg.

Place in a roasting tin and fill with warm water till half way up the mould.

Place in an oven gas 6/200C/400F for about 45 minutes or until just cooked, they should be firm on the top. Remove with a cloth, use a small knife to run round the edge then let the pudding fall into the palm of your hand, quickly place into a serving dish leaving the bread side on top.

Serve with cream.

This is a very light sweet and your guests will be amazed to get individual bread & butter pudding.

Now is the time when hopefully the cold weather is behind us and we can look forward to the coming of spring when new vegetables are beginning to show through and a warmer climate is on its way. March is special for the church with Lent, Ash Wednesday, St. Patrick's Day and Shrove Tuesday when we must think about pancakes. It is also Mothering Sunday in March so there is a lot to think about for our food during this month.

AVOCADO WITH PRAWNS AND PINK GRAPEFRUIT

Prep time: 15 minutes

12 oz / 350g Prawns

3 ripe avocados preferably hass

1 small jar cocktail sauce

1 lemon

1 small lettuce

2 pink grapefruits

1 small jar vinaigrette

Teaspoon Dijon mustard

Segment the grapefruit by taking a thin slice from the top and bottom of the fruit so it can stand on your board without rolling about.

With your knife cut round barrel fashion down the fruit to remove all the pith leaving just the bare fruit. Now hold in your hand, cut between the layers to remove each segment in a bowl and squeeze the remainder to get the juice out.

Wash and dry the lettuce, lay two or three leaves on top of each other and roll up, with a sharp knife shred the lettuce this way. Mix some of the vinaigrette with a teaspoon of Dijon mustard.

Cut the avocados in half length ways and remove the stones, with the point of the knife, trace a line down the centre of the skins and peel the avocados. Place flat down on a chopping board and cut with a stainless steel knife in $1/4$ inch slices leaving about $1/2$ inch at the bottom so the avocado is in one piece then with the palm of your hand gently fan out the avocado.

Wash the prawns well dry and mix with the cocktail sauce place in the centre of a plate place the avocado on top around the plate put the lettuce and sprinkle with the vinaigrette dressing garnish with the grapefruit and slices of lemon.

CAULIFLOWER AND BACON RAMEKIN

Prep time: 25 minutes

Cooking time: 25 minutes

1 cauliflower

6 oz / 175g strong cheddar cheese grated

6 rashers smoked back bacon

1 finely chopped onion

1 pint full cream milk

2 oz / 50g plain flour

2 oz / 50g butter

Top Tip

This can be made in advance and ready for the oven

Cut the cauliflower into florets, cook in salted water for about 20 minutes until almost cooked with just a little dente, then refresh under running cold water till really cold, remove from water allow to drain.

Cut the rashers into slices and fry off with the onion for about 4-5 minutes remove from pan.

Melt the butter in a pan then add the flour to make a roux, cook out for 1 minute gradually add milk stirring all the time with a wooden spoon, if you add the milk too quickly your sauce will become lumpy. The sauce should just coat the back of your spoon, add 4 oz of the cheese and season for taste.

Put portions of cauliflower in the bottom of a ramekin sprinkle over the bacon and onions, cover with the sauce, sprinkle with the rest of the cheese, place on a baking sheet cook in an oven 200C/400F/Gas 6 for about 20-25 minutes serve on a plate with a doily on the bottom.

DUCK CASSEROLE WITH APRICOTS, MINT AND PINE NUTS

Prep time: 15 minutes

Cooking time: 30 minutes

6 duck breasts

Seasoned flour

1 tbsp oil

1 oz / 25g butter

1 large onion sliced

1 pint red wine

3 tbsp red wine vinegar

3 tbsp clear honey

3 oz / 75g ready to eat dried apricots

$1^{1}/_{2}$ oz / 40g pine nuts toasted

4 tbsp chopped fresh mint

Mint leaves to garnish

Wash and wipe the duck breasts, season, and sprinkle with the flour. Heat the butter and oil in an ovenproof casserole; add the duck, fry till a golden brown on each side.

Remove from pan, drain off the fat, add the onion and fry off for about 5 minutes or until softened. Add the red wine, vinegar and honey, then bring to the boil, simmer for 5 minutes. Return the duck breasts, cover and simmer for 10 minutes, skim off any fat, stir in the apricots and pine nuts, cover with a lid and simmer for 15 minutes.

Transfer the duck breasts to keep warm, skim off any fat that settles on top of the sauce, and reduce until it begins to thicken, stir in the chopped mint, and season for taste, and pour sauce over the breasts garnish with mint leaves.

GRILLED LEMONY POTATOES

Prep time: 5 minutes

Cooking time: 25 minutes

1 $1/_2$ lb / 700g potatoes scrubbed and not peeled

2 oz / 50g Melted butter

1 tbsp chopped fresh mint

2 tsp lemon juice

$1/_4$ pint mayonnaise

1 crushed clove of garlic

Cut potatoes into $1/_2$ inch slices, cook in boiling water for 6 minutes, remove and drain.

Line a large dish with foil and lay the potatoes on top, brush with butter and sprinkle with the chopped mint, season. Cook under grill for 5 minutes each side.

Mix the mayonnaise with the garlic and spoon over the sliced potatoes pop under the grill for 2 minutes and serve while still hot.

RED CABBAGE ASASCIENNE

Prep time: 6 minutes

Cooking time: 1 hour

1 red cabbage shredded

1 lb / 450g apples cored and sliced

1 lb / 450g sliced onions

$1/_2$ pint cider or red wine vinegar

4 oz / 100g butter

Prepare the cabbage and shred not too thin. Put the butter in a casserole dish and sweat off the onions without colour, add the apples and mix together. Mix in the cabbage, combine well with the apples and onions, and add the vinegar and season cover with a lid, put in a hot oven Gas 6/200C/400F, leave to cook for at least 1 hour.

This dish will freeze very well.

CARROTS GLACE

Prep time: 8 minutes

Cooking time: 25 minutes

1 $1/_2$ lb / 700g carrots

1 diced onion

2 oz / 100gbutter

1 tbsp clear honey

1 oz / 25g chopped parsley or chives

Peel the carrots and cut into $3/_4$ inch batons, put into a pan cover with cold water season with salt, bring to the boil, put a lid on and cook for about 20 minutes or till the carrots are a bit underdone dente. In another pan sweat off the onions in the butter till just cooked without colour add the honey, drain off the carrots and add to the pan with the onions and honey. Mix well together till fully coated with the glaze, serve in a vegetable dish, sprinkle with the chopped parsley or chives the choice is yours.

BRANDIED FRUITY PANCAKES

Prep time: 12 minutes

Cooking time: 15 minutes

5 oz / 125g plain flour

2 eggs

$^1/_2$ pt milk

$^1/_4$ pt brandy

2 oz / 50g butter

2 oz / 50g castor sugar

1 tbsp of oil

Pinch of salt

Oil for frying

3 Bananas sliced

Chopped fresh fruit

Maple syrup and icing sugar, to serve

Sieve the flour and salt together into a large bowl, add the eggs, pour in a little milk and whisk together gradually till all the milk has been used.

The batter should be the consistency of half whipped cream, beat in the oil and allow to stand for 30 minutes.

Heat a frying pan with some oil, add some bananas and cook a little pour in a little batter swirl around the pan so it is even all over, cook for about 1 minute, flip over with a palette knife and cook the other side. Repeat this till all the pancakes have been finished.

Put the butter in a pan, melt, add the sugar and chopped fresh fruit cook for about 2 minutes add the brandy and maple syrup to make a good fruity sauce.

Place 2 pancakes on each plate and top with the fruit and sauce sprinkle dust with icing sugar.

Top Tip

Make pancakes in advance leave
between grease proof paper reheat
when ready

Spring has arrived, so give your friends a post-winter wake up call by inviting them round to share the first flavours of the season. Our dinner menu makes the most of light and fresh tastes around, combining subtle flavours from tuna on a fresh mixed salad to the succulent new fresh spring cabbage to a light chocolate mousse which will stun your guests. What better for the main course than lamb? Use a lean french cut of rack of lamb that you will find in supermarkets or ask your butcher to prepare one for you.

Overall this menu requires little fuss, but the end results are stunning. Your guests will be glad they came out of hibernation.

HALF A MELON WITH ORANGE AND GINGER

Prep time: 15 minutes

3 ripe medium sized melons

3 medium sized oranges

A little ground ginger

Mint leaves to decorate

Carefully cut the bottom and top of the melon so it will sit comfortably on either end. Round the middle with a small knife zigzag right round being careful to get even cuts all the way round.

Now you have 2 halves do this to all the melons, you should now have the 6 portions.

Remove the pips.

With a round baler (in the trade we call it a noisette cutter) go round the melon and take out all the flesh being careful not to pierce the bottom.

Put all the balls in a bowl, cut the oranges into segments as we have done before with the grapefruit. Put all the segments of orange with the melon and sprinkle with the ginger, place in a refrigerator till ready to serve. Put your melon bases on a plate place the mixture in them and decorate with mint leaves.

Top Tip

This can be made in advance

16

HONEY GLAZED TUNA ON A MIXED SALAD

$1/4$ cup of honey

$1/4$ cup soy sauce

1 tsp toasted sesame seeds

$1/2$ tsp crushed red pepper

6 x 4 oz / 100g tuna steaks
cut about $3/4$ inch thick

12 red cherry tomatoes

1 small lettuce

1 small radicchio

1 bunch watercress

2 spring onions

Rinse the tuna and pat dry. In a bowl mix the honey, soy, sesame seeds and crushed pepper together. Set aside about 2 tbsp of dressing for the salad.

Preheat a grill and brush both sides of the tuna with the dressing, grill until fish flakes easily with a fork.

Allow about 4 minutes either side for grilling. Shred the lettuce and radicchio coarsely, chop up the spring onion and mix together.

Wash the tomatoes and watercress thoroughly and mix with the salad. Arrange on a plate drizzle with a little of the dressing.

Cut tuna across the grain into $1/2$ inch-wide slices arrange on the salad and drizzle over with the sauce.

ROAST RACK OF LAMB

Prep time: 8 minutes
Cooking time: 30 minutes

3 x 12 oz / 350g racks of lamb French trimmed

2 tbsp plain flour

2 tbsp red currant jelly

2 tbsp port

6 fl oz fresh orange juice

10 fl oz vegetable stock

1 tsp dark soy sauce

A little oil

Preheat oven to 220C/ 425F/GAS 7.

Place the lamb in a roasting tin, brush over with a little oil. Roast for 20 minutes to serve pink or 25 minutes if you prefer the lamb well done. Remove the racks from the tin, cover with foil and keep warm.

Put the tin on a medium heat on the stove and stir in the flour to make a smooth paste, stir in the jelly, orange juice and stock, bring to the boil stirring all the time, cook out for 3 minutes until thickened and smooth. Stir in the soy sauce and port then strain.

Cut each rack into 6 cutlets, put 3 cutlets on each plate garnish with watercress.

Strain the sauce and serve in sauce boats.

GARLIC & POTATO PATTIES

Prep time: 5 minutes
Cooking time: 45 minutes

1$^1/_2$lb / 700g potatoes
cooked and mashed

2 tbsp fresh chopped parsley

3 cloves crushed garlic

3 tbsp oil

1 egg yolk

Boil and mash the potatoes but do not put any butter or milk in them.

Preheat the oven to 220C/425F/Gas 7 and slightly grease a baking sheet. Mix the potatoes with the egg yolk, parsley, and crushed garlic, season with salt and black pepper.

Shape into 6 round patties, flatten slightly, and place on the oiled baking sheet. Brush with oil and bake for 15 minutes until crisp and golden brown.

Top Tip

These can be made in advance and ready to bake

GLAZED SHALLOTS

Prep time: 12 minutes

Cooking time: 20 minutes

1 lb / 450g shallots

1 oz / 25g butter

1 tbsp oil

1 tsp sugar

Chopped fresh parsley

Bring a pan of water to the boil, add the shallots, cover and simmer for 3 minutes.

Drain and refresh under cold water, remove the skins, leaving the root intact. Heat the butter and oil in a heavy-based pan, add the sugar and shallots and cook for about 15-20 minutes, shaking the pan several times so the shallots are a nice golden brown.

Season and serve with the chopped parsley.

BRAISED SPRING CABBAGE BALLS

Prep time: 20 minutes

Cooking time: 20 minutes

1$^1/_2$lb / 700g spring cabbage

1 finely chopped onion

$^1/_2$ pint vegetable stock

One glass of a dry white wine

2 oz / 50g butter

Take 6 outer leaves from the cabbage, remove the thick end of the stalk and wash well. Put on a pan of boiling salted water and just before putting in the cabbage leaves add a dessert spoon of sugar, this will keep the cabbage green.

Cook for about 3 minutes then refresh under cold water, remove the leaves when they are cold, place on a clean tea towel and reserve.

In a small pan add the butter, sweat off the onions without colour, add the glass of wine and reduce by half.

Shred the remaining cabbage and cook in boiling salted water for about 10 minutes till nearly cooked but with a bit of a bite to it, drain and allow to cool, then season with salt and pepper, mix well then form into small balls.

Take one of your leaves lay flat on a clean tea towel place one of the cabbage balls in the middle bring up your tea towel and form small balls, squeeze gently to remove any excess water, place in a casserole dish. Do this to all the cabbages till all the leaves have been used. Cover with the stock then cover the dish with foil and place in a heated oven 200C/400F/Gas 6 and cook for 15-20 minutes. Remove the cabbage balls to a serving dish; mask with the reduced white wine.

Top Tip

These can be made in advance and ready for the oven

CHOCOLATE MOUSSE

Prep time: 25 minutes

Chilling time: 4 hours

6 eggs

4 oz / 100g castor sugar

$^1/_2$ pint double cream

8 oz / 200g plain chocolate

1 tbsp Cointreau

Grated zest of one orange

Chocolate leaves see tips

Separate the eggs whisk the yolks with the sugar until pale and creamy. Beat the cream in a bowl until lightly thickened, stir in the yolks and sugar.

Melt the chocolate in a bowl over a pan of warm water make sure you stir occasionally so the chocolate melts evenly. Cool slightly stir into the cream mixture.

Whisk the egg whites until stiff, stir a little into the chocolate mixture, and fold in the rest. Add the cointreau and orange zest.

Spoon into individual dishes and chill for 4 hours. Decorate with chocolate leaves.

Tips: choose well-defined leaves such as rose or bay wash well and dry.

Dip the underside into melted chocolate or paint on with a brush, allow excess to drain back into the bowl.

Place on a baking sheet covered with greaseproof paper, allow to set, when set peel away the leaf, you will now have your chocolate leaf for decoration.

Spring is here, time to really wake up to see that the farmers are busy in the fields where new vegetables are showing their way through the ground. Keep a look out in your supermarkets for these vegetables: baby courgettes, tender asparagus tips and the first morels. Then there is the fresh salmon from the fast flowing rivers in Scotland. Greet the new season with a little spring chicken why not go into your supermarket look at all the new produce and take some home then taste the difference in the flavour and surely you will be amazed how your taste buds will re-act to their flavours

FRESH ASPARAGUS SERVED WITH A CREAMY HOLLANDAISE SAUCE

Prep time: 15 minutes

Cooking time: 6 minutes

36 asparagus tips

1 x $^1/_2$ pint packet hollandaise sauce

4 fl oz lightly whipped double cream

Chopped fresh parsley

Cut off the bottoms of the asparagus, and peel away 2 inches from the bottom up with a potato peeler, tie with string around the bottom to make 6 portions and leave about 6 inches of string overhanging.

Place in boiling salted water with a touch of sugar and simmer for about 6 minutes, leave the strings over hanging your pan, as it is easy to remove each portion without breaking the asparagus.

Drain on a cloth, cut the strings and place on each plate and pour sauce over, sprinkle with chopped parsley.

SAUCE
Make up the hollandaise sauce from the packet, add the parsley, fold in the cream serve while still warm.

ESCALLOP OF WILD SALMON

Prep time: 25 minutes

Cooking time: 3 minutes

$1^{1}/_{2}$ lb / 700g Tail end of salmon

Juice of 1 lemon

4 oz / 100g butter

Little oil

8 young lettuce leaves

4 oz / 100g spinach leaves

24 sorrel leaves

Small bunch chives

2 bunches of water cress

TOMATO BUTTER

1 lb / 450g ripe tomatoes

4 oz / 100g unsalted butter

COOKING THE VEGETABLES

In a pan put a little water no salt, bring to the boil, put in 1 oz of butter, put in the watercress cover with a lid and cook for 4 minutes. Add the spinach and lettuce and cook for a further 2 minutes. Lastly put in the chives and sorrel for a few seconds only, do not over cook or the sorrel will lose its texture. Stir in 2 oz butter season and you could add a dash of white wine vinegar if required. Set aside.

Skin the salmon and carefully take out any small bones with tweezers. Cut into 6 equal portions season and squeeze the lemon juice over them, place in a refrigerator.

Lightly oil a small frying pan add the rest of the butter place in the salmon and seal each one for 10 seconds each side remove, place on a tray then grill for about one minute under a hot grill. The salmon should be barely cooked through, do not over cook or you will ruin the texture and flavour.

TOMATO BUTTER

Put the tomatoes in boiling water for 10 seconds place in cold water, remove the skins, halve and squeeze out the seeds and juice of half of them and cut them into dice and reserve. Puree the rest in a food processor, using a ladle, force through a fine conical sieve into a saucepan.

Warm gently over a low heat, but do not boil, then whisk in the cold-diced butter, add the diced tomatoes taste and season, if the sauce is a bit acidic add a pinch of castor sugar.

Arrange the heated vegetables on a warm plate, carefully place the salmon on top. Finish by masking over with the gently warmed tomato butter.

Garnish with strips of chives.

POUSSIN WITH GRAPES

Prep time: 10 minutes

Cooking time: 60 minutes

6 small poussins

6 rashers rind less back bacon diced

2 cloves garlic crushed

12 fl oz white wine

8 oz / 200g black seedless grapes

6 tbsp brandy

4 tsp corn flour

4 oz / 100g butter

2 tbsp Tomato puree

Fresh Thyme

Heat the butter in a large frying pan, seal the poussins, place in a roasting pan.

In the frying pan add the brandy then ignite and heat till the flames die down add the thyme and pour over the poussins, cover and cook for 45 minutes until they are tender. Set aside and keep warm.

Drain the juices into a saucepan, heat until the juices have reduced, add the bacon and cook till just brown. Add the garlic, tomato puree and mix the white wine with a little of the cornflour, add the rest of the wine to the sauce, thicken with the cornflour.

Halve the grapes add to the sauce taste for flavour and consistency simmer for 5 minutes finish with a little butter to give the sauce a glaze, serve over the poussins.

POTATO AND MUSHROOM MEDLEY

Prep time: 5 minutes

Cooking time: 25 minutes

$1^1/_2$lb / 700g fresh new potatoes

2 oz / 50g butter

Chopped parsley

1 oz / 25g chopped sage

6 oz / 150g button mushrooms

12 shallots

8 fl oz red wine

6 fl oz vegetable stock

Cut the potatoes in half and fry in a large saucepan with the butter and shallots for about 5 minutes, add the wine and stock, season, bring to the boil and simmer for 30 minutes.

Stir in the halved button mushrooms and sage, cook for a further 5 minutes until the potatoes are just cooked and serve in a hot dish, sprinkle with chopped parsley.

STUFFED BABY COURGETTES SERVED ON A BED OF RICE

Prep time: 15 minutes

Cooking time: 35 minutes

6 baby courgettes

12 oz / 350g tomatoes skinned and chopped

4 spring onions chopped

1 clove crushed garlic

4 oz / 100g grated strong cheddar cheese

6 rashers streaky bacon

2oz / 50g long grain rice

Wash the courgettes then lay on a board length ways and cut only a $\frac{1}{4}$ off the top so you can just see the seeds which need removing with a teaspoon.

Chop the top into small dice mix with the spring onion, tomatoes and crushed garlic and cook together until soft.

Meanwhile place the courgettes in an ovenproof dish sprinkle with a few drops of oil place in a heated oven 190C/375F/ Gas 5 for about 15 minutes until the flesh starts to soften. Remove from oven, fill with the tomato mixture, cover with cheese and top with the bacon, place back in the oven for a further 15-20 minutes.

Meanwhile cook the rice in plenty of boiling water until tender, drain then place on a dish serve the stuffed courgettes on top.

BUTTERED MANGE TOUT

Prep time: 8 minutes

Cooking time: 4 minutes

$1\frac{1}{2}$lb / 700g mange tout

2 oz / 50g butter

Salt

Sugar

Wash the mange tout well, top and tail making sure you remove the string on the edges of the vegetable.

Put a pan of salted water on the stove, boil add some sugar, this will help keep the vegetable green, add the mange tout and bring to the boil, simmer for only a few minutes, drain toss in butter and serve.

ZABAGLIONE WITH LANGUES DE CHAT BISCUITS

BISCUITS

Prep time: 15 minutes

Cooking time: 6 minutes

2 oz / 50g butter

2 oz / 50g castor sugar

Finely zest of one orange

2 oz / 50g self-raising flour

2 oz / 50g chocolate, melted

1 egg

Prep time: 3 minutes
Cooking time: 8 minutes

6 egg yolks

3 oz / 75g castor sugar

12 tbsp Marsala wine

Grated chocolate

Orange zest to decorate

FOR THE BISCUITS
Preheat an oven 220C/425F/Gas 7.

Grease and line 2 baking sheets. Cream the butter and sugar until pale and fluffy. Beat in the egg and orange zest, then add the flour until the mixture has a thick piping consistency. Put in a piping bag and pipe fingers about 2 inches long and spaced about 2 inches apart, bake in oven for about 5 minutes until pale golden colour.

Transfer biscuits to a cooling rack.

Dip each end of the biscuits into melted chocolate, leave to set on baking parchment.

TO MAKE THE ZABAGLIONE
Put the egg yolks, sugar and marsala into a large bowl.

Leave this in the fridge covered over till you are ready to make this dessert as it must be made to order. Stir over a pan of simmering water and whisk for about 8 minutes until thick and fluffy, pour the mixture into wine glasses, top with grated chocolate and rind, serve immediately.

This is a very tasty and light dessert.

Note: You can use sherry instead of the Marsala if desired.

Note
This dessert has to be made and served immediately or it will separate, the biscuits can be made during the day.

The season of warmth a heightened display of colour and ripeness prevail. There is no shyness left. Nature proudly displays all its richess. The colours are vivid now. There is a definite statement, a clear taste from matured, ripe fruit and vegetables. There is an overwhelming choice and abundance of vegetables, bursting with full flavour-sunripe tomatoes, the finest soft fruits with their glowing colours. Cookery programmes on television have introduced new produce and foreign cuisine to all of us. These ingredients are now available across the country, either from local shops or specialist mail-order suppliers. Their growing interest in food and cookery is evident in the large range to be found in every supermarket. There is a real sense of satisfaction in putting together a meal that perfectly suits the occasion, the season and the people who are going to eat it.

BAKED GOATS CHEESE AND VEGETABLE PYRAMIDS WITH LEMON AND WALNUT VINAIGRETTE

VINAIGRETTE

2 tbsp walnut oil

1 tsp Dijon mustard

Juice of 1 lemon

Chopped chives

Seasoning

Prep time: 45 minutes

Cooking time: 10 minutes

6 button mushrooms

1 red, yellow and green pepper

1 medium courgette

2 small aubergines

2 medium tomatoes

6 oz / 175g goat's cheese

VINAIGRETTE

Blend the lemon juice, mustard, salt and pepper in a liquidiser, slowly add the oil while the machine is running, add the chopped chives and blend till smooth. Chill until required.

Wash all the vegetables and thoroughly dry. Cut the aubergines in $1/4$ inch slices and place on a plate, sprinkle with salt then place another plate on top, leave for I hour, this will get rid of the bitter juices which are in aubergines. Cut the peppers in half and remove the pips wash and dry then place flat down and place under a hot grill till the skins start to go black, remove and place to one side till cool enough to remove the skins completely.

With a 2 inch round pastry cutter, cut out all the peppers and brush with the vinaigrette. Cut the tomatoes $1/4$ inch thick, brush with vinaigrette. Cut the courgettes $1/4$ inch thick and brush with vinaigrette and cook under a hot grill for 1 minute each side, repeat this with the aubergines.

Layer in stacks on a baking tray with the aubergine at the bottom, followed by the tomato, then some goats cheese, make sure that the base is secure. Top again with yellow, green and red pepper then some more goat's cheese, finish with the courgette and top with the button mushroom.

Make sure the stacks are quite secure sprinkle with the vinaigrette and cook in a pre-heated oven 200C/400F/Gas 6 for 7-8 minutes until heated through. Serve on a plate, drizzle round the dressing.

Top Tip
These can be made in advance and ready for the oven

CHICKEN, SPINACH AND SMOKED BACON ROULADE WITH CUMBERLAND SAUCE

CUMBERLAND SAUCE

Prep time: 20 minutes

Juice of 1 lemon & orange

Small jar redcurrant jelly

1 tbsp brandy

Powdered ginger

Prep time: 20 minutes
Cooking time: 20 minutes

6 small chicken breasts

6 rashers smoked back bacon

6 oz / 175g fresh spinach

$^1/_4$ pint fresh double cream

Seasoning

Remove the zest from the lemon and orange with a potato peeler, cut finely into strips blanch in boiling water for about three minutes, refresh under cold water, drain and set aside. Put the juices into a pan and reduce by half, add the jelly, brandy and ginger, simmer together till the jelly has dissolved, add the strips of rind and allow to cool.

Wash the chicken breasts and dry, then remove the fillet which is just under the breast and will come away quite easily. Wash the spinach and cook in boiling salted water for about 3 minutes, strain and allow cooling, then squeezing out the excess water and make into balls.

Put the fillets into a liquidiser with a blade attachment and mince up the fillets, then add the spinach balls, season then slowly add the cream till a mousse like mixture has formed. Take the breasts and cut open with a sharp knife to make a pocket so that the mixture can be inserted.

When open, put in the mixture then a rasher of bacon and roll up. Place on a piece of cling film and rollup then roll again in some foil and seal each end. Cook in a steamer for about 15-20 minutes and allow to cool.

Remove foil and cling film then slice and lie on a plate, can be served with a little salad. Serve the sauce separately.

Top Tip
These can be made ready in advance

LAMB FILLETS IN FILO PASTRY
SERVED WITH TOMATO, MINT & COURGETTE SALSA

SALSA

Prep time: 12 minutes

4 tomatoes

8 oz / 225g small courgettes finely diced

2 tsp chopped fresh mint

1 shallot finely diced

4 tbsp balsamic vinegar

4 tbsp olive oil

MARINADE

Prep time: 6 minutes

3 tbsp balsamic vinegar

1 tbsp clear honey

1 tbsp chopped fresh rosemary

Mint sprigs

Prep time: 25 minutes

Cooking time: 20 minutes

3 best end necks of lamb weighing about
1 $\frac{1}{4}$lb / 575g each they need to be boned

Use the bones to make a stock for the
Boulangere Potatoes

1 medium leek

12 filo pastry sheets,

1 egg beaten

2 tbsp sesame seeds toasted

Oil

Peel the tomatoes by immersing them in boiling water for 10 seconds then plunging them into cold water. Take off the skins, which should remove easily.

Cut courgettes in half and remove the seeds, cut into dice. Combine the rest of the ingredients season and chill.

Combine all the ingredients for the marinade, put into a bowl. Add the lamb pieces, chill for 24 hours turning occasionally so the lamb takes on the flavour of the marinade.

Heat enough oil in a frying pan and seal the lamb pieces until browned on all sides, transfer to dish to cool.

Blanch the leek leaves by dipping them into boiling salted water until wilted, drain on a dry tea towel. Wrap a piece of leek round each piece of lamb.

Brush the sheets of filo with a little oil and wrap each piece of lamb with 4 layers of pastry. If not cooking immediately, cover with cling film and set aside.

Pre heat the oven 200C/400F/Gas 6. Brush each filo parcel with egg, sprinkle with the sesame seeds. Place on baking sheet and cook in oven for 12-15 minutes for rare or 18-20 minutes for well done, remove and allow to rest for about 3-4 minutes.

Cut each into four, put 2 slices on each plate and drizzle round the salsa, garnish with mint leaves.

BOULANGERE POTATOES

Prep time: 12 minutes

Cooking time: 60 minutes

1¹/₂ lb / 600g potatoes

1 large onion very thinly sliced

1 clove garlic crushed

2 oz / 50g butter

¹/₂ pt stock made from the lamb bones

Seasoning

Put the garlic and butter into the stock, bring to the boil and remove. Peel the potatoes and slice thinly.

Grease an ovenproof dish, arrange a layer of potatoes on the bottom, season, add a layer of onions, and then add a layer of potatoes overlapping in slices.

Add the boiling stock and press down firmly, they should be nearly covered with the stock.

Cook in an oven for at least one hour, or until the potatoes are tender and browned on top. Note to keep your eye on them while cooking. Press down the top whilst cooking to keep the top moist and not too crusty.

FRESH GREEN BEANS WRAPPED IN BACON

Prep time: 15 minutes

Cooking time: 20 minutes

1 lb / 450g thin green beans

6 rashers of back bacon

¹/₄ pt vegetable stock

Wash, top and tail the beans, cook in boiling salted water for about 7-8 minutes until nearly cooked, refresh under cold water.

Place in 6 bundles on a board, wrap a rasher of bacon round each bundle.

Butter an ovenproof dish, place the bundles in the dish, pour in the stock, cover with foil and bake in an oven for about 15 minutes remove the foil and cook for a further 4 minutes to allow the bacon to crisp a little.

Top Tip
These can be made ready in advance ready for the oven

JUNE

GOLDEN TOP CAULIFLOWER

Prep time: 20 minutes

Cooking time: 20 minutes

6 good cauliflower florets

2 eggs hard-boiled

6 tbsp fresh white breadcrumbs

2 oz / 50g butter

Chopped parsley

Separate the eggs into whites and yolks. Finely chop the whites and put the yolks through a sieve.

Melt the butter in a pan and fry the breadcrumbs until golden brown, remove from heat, add the parsley, egg whites and yolks and season.

Boil the cauliflower till tender but crisp arrange in a dish sprinkle with the breadcrumb mixture.

GRAND MARNIER AND APRICOT ALASKA

Prep time: 18 minutes

Cooking time: 6 minutes

$1^3/_4$ pints firm vanilla ice cream [not soft scoop]

2 lb / 900g fresh apricots

8 oz / 225g Madeira cake

5 tbsp grand Marnier

3 egg whites

6 oz / 175g castor sugar

1 orange sliced

Mint leaves

Cut the Madeira cake into 1 inch slices and sprinkle on the Grand Marnier. Line a 1lb loaf tin with cling film, press in the ice cream making sure it does not defrost, leaving 1 inch at the top, place the cake on top and put in the freezer till totally frozen again.

Do this two days in advance, after day one remove the ice cream and sponge from the mould by putting the mould in hot water to loosen the edges. Cling film again and replace in the freezer. Stew the apricots in a little water for about 20 minutes until soft.

Once cooked, allow to cool before discarding the stones and pureeing in a food processor. Preheat the oven to Gas 8/230C/450F. Whisk the egg whites stiffly, add the sugar slowly whisking continuously until the mixture is thick and glossy.

Turn the ice cream onto an oven proof serving dish, cover completely with the meringue using a piping bag. Bake in the oven for about 5 minutes or until just turning brown. Take out of the oven place a little of the puree on top and garnish with the orange and lemon.

You can use any soft fruit with this recipe such as strawberries and raspberries by putting them on top of the meringue when taken out of the oven and using some as a sauce on the plate.

Well you are now into the middle of the year and by now quite familiar with your entertaining and hopefully very successful. One thing I have not mentioned is decoration on your table and a small flower arrangement is very acceptable, it does not need to be too tall as your guests will find it difficult to converse at the table. Think of the flowers in season at that time and look at your colour scheme. My wife Gill does all our arrangements while I am banned to the kitchen. Wines to serve with your meal is a very important factor when entertaining and it is good to check with your guests before hand to understand their tastes then compile a menu to suit, though I am a believer in enjoying food and wine which personally suits me and do not really go for any convential trends. Summer is now here and we must look at cold soups and light meals to go with the weather, or even eat outside depending on the weather in this country.

GAZPACHO

Prep time: 20 minutes

2 lb / 900g plum tomatoes
skinned and de-seeded

1 medium cucumber
peeled and de-seeded

1 small chopped onion

3 cloves garlic, crushed

6 red peppers, seeded and chopped

4 fl oz sherry vinegar

Liquidise all the above ingredients, pass through a fine conical strainer and season add a little Tabasco to taste.

Gazpacho is delicious on its own or served with croutons but can also be served with prawns or a vegetable mousse served in the centre, but this is up to yourself. Serve this soup chilled.

SCAMPI HARLEQUIN WITH RICE

Prep time: 6 minutes
Cooking time: 25 minutes

$1^1/_4$ lb / 500g large scampi

1 small carrot cut into diamond shapes

$^1/_2$ small leek cut into diamond shapes

2 tomatoes skinned
and deseeded cut as above

2 cloves garlic crushed

2 oz / 50g butter

1 oz / 25g plain flour

4 floz single cream

$^1/_2$ pint Dry white wine

Chopped parsley

$^1/_2$ finely chopped onion

Cooked rice

Melt butter in a pan, add the garlic and onions and sweat without colour for 2-3 minutes until the onions are soft.

Dry off the scampi and mix with the flour, add to the onions, fry together for three minutes to seal the scampi, add the carrots and leeks, sweat together then add the white wine and cook out for about 4 minutes, season.

Add the cream and finely add the tomatoes and parsley, if you would like to get an extra sheen on the sauce, finish with some more butter, serve on as bed of rice, garnish with carrot and leek strips.

BEEF ENCROUTE

Prep time: 25 minutes

Cooking time: 30-40 minutes

2 lb / 900g rolled beef fillet

2 tsp chopped fresh thyme

2 tsp strong mustard

1 egg beaten

1$^1/_4$ lb / 500g puff pastry

8 large slices smoked cooked ham

4 oz / 100g spinach,
chopped cooked and well drained

Quickly seal the meat in a hot frying pan, season, and spread with mustard, sprinkle with the thyme.

Roll out pastry long and wide enough to wrap the meat completely, you will need a $^3/_4$ inch overlap for the seal. Lay 4 slices of ham in the centre of the pastry and place half the spinach on top, followed by the beef.

Put the remaining spinach and ham on top of the beef. Use one hand to hold the ham and spinach on top and the other to wrap pastry around the beef as tight as possible.

Brush the two edges with the egg and seal roll the beef over so the sealed end is on the baking sheet. Preheat the oven to 230C/450F/Gas 8, cook the beef for medium rare 20-30 minutes or well done, 35-40 minutes.

Allow relaxing for 3-4 minutes before carving. Cover with foil if the pastry is becoming too dark before the meat is ready.

NORMANDE POTATOES

Prep time: 10 minutes

Cooking time: 20 minutes

2 lb / 900g potatoes
peeled and cut in slices

4 oz / 100g white of leek

1 shredded onion

2 oz / 50g butter

1 oz / 25g plain flour

$^1/_2$ pint milk

4 oz / 100g grated cheddar cheese

Sweat the leek and onion in the butter for about 3 minutes, add the flour, mix together thoroughly and pour in the milk slowly to absorb the roux.

Place in the sliced potatoes bring to the boil cook for about 5 minutes, place in an earthen-ware dish, sprinkle with cheese, place in a preheated oven 200C/400F/Gas 6 for about 15-20 minutes by then the potatoes should be creamy with a nice crusty cheese top.

CELERY ALMONDINE

Prep time: 8 minutes

Cooking time: 30 minutes

3 heads of trimmed celery hearts

1 chopped onion

3 oz / 75g butter

3 oz / 75g plain flour

2 tbsp single cream

6 oz / 150g toasted flaked almonds

Wash and trim the celery, cut into strips across the grain put in a pan cover with water and cook for 15 minutes or until the celery is tender.

Strain and keep the liquor separately in a pan, then reduce to about 3/4 pint. Cook the onions with the butter for about 4 minutes until soft but without colour, stir in the flour, mix thoroughly add the celery liquor and cream till you have a creamy sauce.

Add the celery mix with half the almonds and put in an ovenproof dish; sprinkle the rest of the almonds on top, place in a preheated oven 200C/400F/Gas 6 for approximately 10 minutes.

ORIENTAL SALAD

DRESSING

Prep time: 4 minutes

6 tbsp oil

3 tbsp white wine vinegar

2 cloves crushed garlic

3 tbsp soy sauce

To make the dressing put all the ingredients into a jar put the lid on and shake vigorously to blend, and then set aside.

Prep time: 15 minutes

1/2 cucumber

1 red pepper

1 yellow pepper

1-bunch spring onions

12 oz / 350g bean sprouts

4 tbsp toasted sesame seeds

Cut the cucumber in half length ways and scoop out the seeds. Cut in half down the middle again and cut into strips.

Remove the seeds from the peppers, cut into quarters and slice. Wash the spring onion, slice and mix with the peppers and cucumber, add the bean sprout and toss together.

Pour over the dressing and toss the salad gently. Chill for 1 hour or up to 5 hours. Add the toasted sesame seeds just before serving and toss again.

JULY

RASPBERRIES IN A WINE JELLY

Prep time: 35 minutes

1 bottle Rosé wine

2 tbsp Bristol Cream sherry

$1/4$ lb / 100g castor sugar

8 leaves gelatine

2 punnets raspberries

$1/2$ pint double cream

Place the wine and sugar in a pan and bring to the boil to dissolve the sugar.

Put the gelatine in cold water to let it go limp and pliable, this may take about 10 minutes, add to the wine, stir slowly and add the sherry, allow to cool.

Pour $1/2$ inch of jelly into each individual mould, put in fridge and allow them to set. Wash the fruit and drain well, then put some raspberries in the bottom, top with a little jelly, allow them to set.

Repeat this till the moulds are full. Chill them until thoroughly set. To serve, turn out onto a plate and decorate with a sprig of fresh mint, serve cream separately.

Note

Make this a day before and keep in the refrigerator.

Well Summer is here and we all like to think of those holidays in the sun where we can get a tan and remember those days when we had exotic meals in the sun. Just imagine a week in Sicily, each morning the market traders set up their stalls of gleaming fresh fish, newly picked vegetables and bunches of herbs. The fresh fruit which we buy and eat on the beach or take back to our apartments or hotel and can't you remember that succulent taste, oh yes. So your guests have had there holidays and what a surprise when you present them with a Sicilian Meal.

ARANCINI DI RISO

Prep time: 45 minutes

Cooking time: 12 minutes

3 oz / 75g butter

1 onion finely chopped

$1/4$ pint dry white wine

$9^1/_2$ oz / 235g Italian risotto rice

$1^3/_4$ pint chicken stock

1 oz / 25g freshly grated Parmesan cheese

2 eggs

$3^1/_2$ oz / 90g dried white bread crumbs

Oil for deep-frying

$3^1/_2$ oz / 90g mozzarella

Melt butter in a large pan add the onions and cook gently, until soft but not coloured. Pour in the wine and reduce until it has almost evaporated.

Stir in rice and thoroughly mix to coat, add stock slowly to absorb the rice until all the stock has been used, season and cook for 20 minutes the rice should be cooked but have a slight bite, stir in the parmesan, allow to cool. Beat the eggs together, add to the cold rice.

Cut the mozzarella into tiny cubes. Take a small spoonful of rice on your the palm of your wet hand lay a cube of mozzarella in the centre, take some more rice and place on top to completely enclose to make small balls.

Continue to make small balls until all the rice has been used up. Put the breadcrumbs into a bowl roll the rice balls in them till completely covered.

Heat the oil till 180C/350F/Gas 4. Fry in batches for 3-5 minutes until golden brown, drain and serve immediately.

Can be served with a small salad and vinaigrette to suit.

PASTA TRAMPANESE

Prep time: 12 minutes

Cooking time: 12 minutes

3 ripe tomatoes skinned

4 garlic cloves

2oz / 50g basil leaves

3$^{1}/_{2}$ oz / 90g blanched almonds

$^{1}/_{4}$ pint olive oil

1 lb / 450g bucatini [spaghetti-like pasta]

3 tomatoes, seeded and diced

Few almonds

Chopped basil to garnish

Place the 3 ripe tomatoes, garlic, basil leaves almonds and oil in a food processor and blend until smooth.

Cover and chill in the fridge.

Bring a large pan of salted water to the boil and cook pasta until tender, drain well and toss the pasta with the pesto as the Italians do, so the pasta absorbs the flavours.

Season and serve garnished with diced tomatoes almonds and basil.

FARSUMAGRU

STUFFING

Prep time: 10 minutes

7 oz / 175g minced beef

7 oz / 175g minced pork

2 oz / 50g fresh white breadcrumbs

5 cloves garlic crushed

2 tbsp chopped fresh parsley

2 tbsp grated Parmesan

1 egg

Prep time: 15 minutes

Cooking time: 1 hour 30 minutes

2 lb / 900g topside or rump

7 oz / 175g streaky bacon

2 tbsp seasoned flour

2 tbsp olive oil

$\frac{1}{2}$ pint red wine

1oz / 25g butter

1 tin / 400g chopped tomatoes

STUFFING
Mix all the ingredients very well together.

Preheat the oven to 180C/ 350F/ Gas 5.

Cut the meat almost in half horizontally and open out [called butter flying] spread the meat out on a sheet of cling film, beat out with a rolling pin until about 1cm thick, cover with the bacon.

Spread the stuffing mixture over the bacon leaving a border all around. Roll up the meat like a Swiss roll and tie neatly at intervals along the roll.

Sprinkle the seasoned flour over a work surface and roll the meat in it.

Heat the oil and butter in a flameproof casserole, add the beef and seal all over till brown. Add the wine and tin of chopped tomatoes, cover tightly with a lid, cook in the oven for 1 hour 30 minutes till tender.

Remove from pan and reduce the liquor to a sauce, strain, serve in a sauce boat.

Cut the beef when rested into thick slices

CAPONATA

Prep time: 15 minutes

Cooking time: 30 minutes

4 medium aubergines, diced

1 lb / 400g chopped tomatoes

1 onion chopped

1 tbsp capers

2 oz / 50g green olives

3 tbsp red wine vinegar

Olive oil for frying

1 tbsp sugar

Toasted chopped almonds

Chopped fresh parsley

Place the aubergines in a colander, sprinkle with salt and leave to absorb for 30 minutes.

Rinse, pat dry then fry in olive oil in batches till golden brown, drain well and allow to cool.

Heat a little olive oil in a pan add the onion, cook without colour for 5 minutes, add the tomatoes and cook for about 15 minutes until the mixture becomes pulpy.   Add the capers, olives, vinegar and sugar and cook for a further 15 minutes.

Season add the aubergines and stir well, allow to stand for about 30 minutes for the flavours to develop.

Serve warm or cold in a bowl topped with toasted almonds and parsley.

Top Tips

This can be made in advance and topped with toasted almonds before serving

SICILIAN PEACHES

Prep time: 10 minutes

Cooking time: 15 minutes

Sauce: 30 minutes

5 oz / 125g castor sugar

1 bottle of Italian red wine

Juice and zest of 1 orange

6 x 7oz / 175g fresh ripe peaches

2 oz / 50g shelled pistachio nuts

12 fresh strawberries

Peel the zest from the orange and cut into strips, blanch in boiling water, refresh.

Place the red wine, sugar and orange juice in a large pan and stir over a gentle heat until the sugar has dissolved, increase the heat and boil for 5 minutes.

Reduce the heat and poach the peaches for 12 minutes or until just tender. Remove with a slotted spoon, set-aside until cool, carefully peel off the skins while still warm.

Simmer the sauce for a further 30 minutes until thickened. Meanwhile pour boiling water over the pistachios and leave for 5 minutes, strain and slip off the skins to reveal the green nuts.

Place peaches on a plate a few washed strawberries by the side of the peaches drizzle over with the sauce and sprinkle with the pistachios top the peach with the orange zest.

Note
Make this the day before

SEPTEMBER

The basic objective of any meal is that it should taste good. Anything else should spring from that notion or be secondary to it. Considerations of colour, presentation and such like are only important once true flavours have been achieved. Use your own taste buds as a measure of progress and success, not any perceptions of what's expected. Most of all, ask yourself, if the answer is yes, then you will have one satisfied diner at least. This month you have plenty of game birds to choose from with Grouse, Snipe, Partridge and Wild Duck, though most game needs to be hung to tenderise the meat and allow the gamey flavour to develop. Supermarket birds are oven ready and packaging should carry information about their age, be sure to check the 'best before date', and refer to the cooking instructions.

SMOKED SALMON MOUSSE

Prep time: 15 minutes

Cooking time: 12 minutes

12 oz / 350g smoked salmon sliced and trimmed

Juice of $^1/_2$ lemon

$^3/_4$ pint whipping cream

3 pinches of cayenne pepper

Combine the salmon, lemon juice and cayenne pepper in a food processor and puree for 2 minutes only.

With the food processor at its slowest speed, slowly add half the chilled whipping cream, refrigerate for 15 minutes.

In a large bowl whip the remainder of the cream to a light peak and fold into the salmon puree, cutting and lifting with a spoon. Leave in a refrigerator for at least 3 hours.

Serving take two dessert spoons dipped into warm water, shape the mousse into quenelles, arranging 3 portions on each plate.

Serve with a small salad and slices of toast cut into fingers with lemon wedges.

Note
This can be made well in advance

41

TOMATO JELLY WITH LAYERS OF SMOKED HAM
SERVED WITH A HORSERADISH VINAIGRETTE

Prep time: 20 minutes

1 pint of tomato juice

Juice of $^1/_2$ lemon

$^1/_2$ tsp Worcestershire sauce

3 tbsp dry sherry

Dash of Tabasco

5 sheets of gelatine

4 oz / 100g smoked ham

HORSERADISH VINAIGRETTE

1tsp Horseradish sauce

4 tbsp olive oil

2 tbsp white wine vinegar

Chopped parsley

Put the gelatine in a bowl, cover with cold water, and leave till it softens. Pour the tomato juice, lemon juice and Tabasco into a saucepan, bring to the boil stirring all the time.

Remove from the heat, add the gelatine and stir till it has dissolved. Stir in the sherry and put in a clean bowl, pour a little into six individual moulds and allow to set in the fridge, then put a piece of ham on top. When set repeat the process till you have three layers of tomato jelly and ham.

Leave to set overnight in the fridge.

Put all the ingredients in a mixer and thoroughly mix, taste for flavour and adapt to your own requirements by adding more oil, vinegar or horseradish to suit.

Dip each mould quickly in hot water and invert on to a serving plate, serve a little salad on each plate and drizzle round the vinaigrette.

Top Tip
This dish can be made well in advance

ROAST GROUSE WITH BLACKBERRY SAUCE

Prep time: 5 minutes

Cooking time: 20 minutes

6 x 12 oz / 350g grouse

4 oz / 100g unsalted butter

3 tsp oil

SAUCE

Prep time: 5 minutes

Cooking time: 10 minutes

6 oz / 150g ripe blackberries

1 oz / 25g butter

2 tbsp red wine vinegar

5 fl oz port

3 fl oz red wine

8 fl oz chicken stock

GARNISH

30 ripe fresh blackberries and watercress

Get your butcher to truss up the bird so it is ready for the oven and make sure it is fresh and has not been hung for more than two days.

Wash the bird before cooking, dry and season.

In a large frying pan, heat the butter and oil until hot, put the birds on their thighs and seal for 30 seconds each side. Lay them on their backs and cook in a preheated oven 200C/400F/Gas 6 for 12-15 minutes.

Leave to rest for 5 minutes cut down the centre of the breast to remove the carcass, and then keep the rest of the bird warm ready to serve.

Chop the carcass and blend with the residue from the cooking liquid, add the wine vinegar, port, red wine and chicken stock, bring to the boil and simmer.   In the meantime puree the blackberries in a blender and add to the liquid, simmer for another 5 minutes.

Strain through a fine sieve into a small saucepan, press as much juice of the liquid through so as to get the flavour.

Season to taste and if you feel the sauce is a little thin for you thicken with a little corn flour, bring to the boil and finish the sauce with the butter to give a nice glaze.

To serve slice the breasts in two, cut the legs at the thigh joints, arrange around the plates.

Add the whole blackberries to the sauce simmer for 1 minute, pour some over the grouse garnish with the watercress.

CHILLI ROAST POTATOES

Prep time: 12 minutes

Cooking time: 45 minutes

2 lb / 900g old potatoes all the same size if possible

Dripping or lard

1 tsp chilli powder

1 tbsp shredded basil

Peel the potatoes into barrel shapes all about the same size, place into cold salted water, bring to the boil, simmer for 8 minutes, and drain in a colander.

Pre-heat oven 200C/400F/Gas 6 place fat in a roasting tin to get hot, add potatoes and quickly seal all over, place in oven cook for 20 minutes.

Turn over, add the chilli powder and allow to cook for a further 15 minutes. Pour off the fat, cook for a further 15 minutes till a golden brown, season with salt, add the basil, and serve immediately.

BROCCOLI POLONAISE

Prep time: 5 minutes

Cooking time: 20 minutes

6 florets of broccoli

2 hard-boiled eggs

3 oz / 75g fresh white breadcrumbs

2 oz / 50g freshly chopped parsley

4 oz / 100g butter

Cook florets in boiling salted water. Meanwhile melt the butter in a frying pan and add the breadcrumbs, mix together till a golden brown, add the parsley.

Put the egg white and yolk through a sieve then at the last minute add to the breadcrumbs.

When the broccoli is cooked put in a serving dish then cover with the breadcrumb mixture serve piping hot.

FILO BOATS FILLED

WITH LEEK PUREE

Prep time: 20 minutes

Cooking time: 30 minutes

6 sheets of filo pastry

3 oz / 75g melted butter

LEEK PUREE

12 oz / 300g leeks trimmed

2 oz / 50g butter

2 tbsp chicken stock

1 tbsp freshly chopped parsley

Seasoning

Chopped chives

Cut a template from some greaseproof paper about $1/2$ inch larger all round the top of a mould.

Place this on the filo pastry and use as a guide to cut out 36 shapes. Brush each one with melted butter and line each mould with the filo pastry. You will need 12 moulds and three layers in each mould.

Press the pastry well into each mould then trim the edges with scissors so they are neat. Place the moulds on a baking sheet and bake in an oven for 5-8 minutes.

LEEK PUREE
Slice the leeks very finely, heat the butter and stock in a pan, add the leeks, cover with a lid and cook over a gentle heat for about 10 minutes or until the leeks are tender.

Add the chopped parsley.

Puree in a food processor for a few seconds, season for taste. Spoon the hot puree into the boats and sprinkle with the chopped chives, serve immediately.

CARAMELISED RICE PUDDING AND ORANGES
WITH A GINGER CARAMELISED SAUCE

Prep time: 8 minutes

Cooking time: 70 minutes

4 oz / 100g pudding rice

3 egg yolks

1pt Milk

5 oz / 125g caster sugar

$1/4$ pint single cream

Zest of 2 oranges

2 tbsp Grand Marnier

CARAMEL GINGER SAUCE

Prep time: 10 minutes

Cooking time: 8 minutes

1 inch piece of fresh ginger root peeled and chopped

5 oz / 125g sugar

2 oz / 50g butter

4 large oranges

4 fl oz water

2 kiwi fruit

Wash the rice and drain well. Put the rice, sugar and milk in a pan and heat over a gentle heat and simmer for 35 minutes, stirring all the time to prevent it sticking.

Taste to see if it is cooked and sweet enough, add the zest and Grand Marnier and mix well. When cold add the egg yolks and cream, again taste for flavour.

Butter and sugar 6 ramekin moulds, divide the rice between them, place in a roasting tray, add warm water in the tray to come half way up the moulds, this is called a 'Bain Marie' bake in an oven 200C/400F/Gas 6 for about 30 minutes until set.

Segment the oranges and keep in a bowl but strain off any juice into a jug.

Peel and slice the kiwi fruit. Put the ginger and sugar in a small pan with the water and cook over a medium heat until caramelised, add the orange juice and butter, allow to cook for about 3 minutes till a thick syrup has formed and a light golden colour, remove from heat and put the base into cold water to stop the cooking process.

To serve turn out the rice on the middle of the plate spoon over the top the caramel sauce, put segments of orange and kiwi fruit round the plate to garnish and drizzle a little sauce over the segments.

Top Tip

This dish can be prepared in advance which will save you a lot of time on the day

You have by now got quite accustomed to entertaining your guests and they in turn have enjoyed the food you have served up to them. But what we have not touched on is the wine we serve with each meal, though I have said serve the wine you like with each course. Your guests will like to know a little about each wine so I advise you to do a little home work on the wines you serve and I am sure they will be impressed with your knowledge.

TWICE BAKED CHEESE AND BACON SOUFFLE
WITH A ROASTED RED PEPPER SAUCE

Prep time: 5 minutes

Cooking time: 15 minutes

SAUCE

1 crushed clove of garlic

1 finely chopped shallot

1 tbsp oil

4 ripe tomatoes

4 fl oz vegetable stock

2 red peppers

1oz / 25g butter

Prep time: 12 minutes

Cooking time: 12 minutes

SOUFFLE

2 oz / 50g grated Parmesan cheese

2oz / 50g Grated Cheddar Cheese

1 oz / 25g butter

2 tbsp plain flour

8 fl oz milk

5 eggs, yolks separated from the whites

6 oz / 150g back bacon

Chopped parsley

SAUCE
Sweat together in a pan the oil garlic and onions until soft not brown. Put the tomatoes in boiling water for 10 seconds remove into cold water, peel off the skins cut in half and remove the pips, wash and chop, add to the onions and cook out for 5 minutes.

Bake the peppers in a preheated oven for about 10 minutes till dark spots appear on the skins, remove and cover for 3-4 minutes. Remove the skins, take out the seeds and chop finely.

Add the stock and peppers to your pan and cook for about 5 minutes until soft. Transfer the mixture to a blender and puree. Return to pan and season for taste correct the consistency add the butter to give the sauce a glaze and allow to cool. This sauce can be served hot or cold.

SOUFFLE
Butter or oil a Swiss roll tin 13 inches by 10 inches, line it with greaseproof paper, butter or oil the paper. Melt the butter in a pan over a medium heat and stir in the flour and mix with a wooden spoon for about 2 minutes, do not let it brown.

Slowly add the milk stirring all the time until the mixture thickens and there are no lumps. Remove from the heat and put a lid on the pan, so a skin does not form, leave for about 8-10 minutes.

Beat in the egg yolks one at a time till thoroughly mixed. Beat up the egg whites till stiff, stir in a third, fold in the Parmesan Cheese till completely mixed. Spread the mixture in the prepared tin bake in a preheated oven180C/350F/Gas 4 for 15 minutes.

Meanwhile grill the bacon, slice into strips and reserve. Remove the roll from the oven and turn onto a clean tea towel, remove the greaseproof paper, sprinkle over the bacon and parsley.

Roll up the souffle, using the tea towel to protect it from direct pressure, start the roll with as tight a fold as possible to avoid a gap in the centre. Carefully slide the roll onto a buttered ovenproof dish making sure that the open side is underneath.

SERVING THE ROLLED SOUFFLE
Preheat oven180C/350F/Gas 4. Brush the souffle with melted butter and sprinkle with Cheddar Cheese place in the oven and heat for about 10-12 minutes, when hot cut into slices and serve on plates.

Pour a little sauce on to the plate to give a bit of colour, serve the rest in a sauce boat.

WARM SALAD OF RED MULLET SERVED WITH A LEMON BALM DRESSING

47

DRESSING

Prep time: 8 minutes

4 tbsp walnut oil

4 tbsp white wine vinegar

$1/2$ small onion finely chopped

1 tbsp chopped lemon balm leaves

Seasoning

SALAD

10 oz / 275g mixed salad leaves such as radicchio, watercress and endive

Prep time: 8 minutes
Cooking time: 25 minutes

2 red mullet
each weighing about 8 oz / 200g cleaned

4 sprigs lemon balm

$1/4$ pint dry white wine

Little oil

TO MAKE THE DRESSING
In a small pan add the liquid from the fish and combine the walnut oil, vinegar and onion and bring to the boil and reduce by half and keep warm until required.

Remove the hard scales from the red mullet place on a board and by holding the tail firmly run a knife along the length of the fish from tail to head.

Rinse and pat dry with kitchen paper. Place a large piece of foil on a tray, cover with greaseproof, lay the fish down the middle add the lemon balm, sprinkle with the white wine, fold over the foil to make a loose parcel.

Bake in an oven 200C/400FGas 6 for about 20 minutes until the fish is cooked and flakes easily. Strain off the liquid and reserve for the dressing.

Carefully remove the bones and skin from the fish, a pair of clean tweezers is ideal to remove the bones. Reserve the fish and keep warm.

Wash the salad leaves and tear into bite size pieces and arrange on the plates with the flaked fish.

Mix in the chopped lemon balm leaves to the dressing and drizzle over the fish and salad serve immediately.

Top Tip

The fish can be prepared for the oven in advance

PHEASANT BREASTS WITH GRAPES AND MUSHROOMS

Prep time: 15 minutes

Cooking time: 15 minutes

Sauce time: 18 minutes

3 pheasants

2 tbsp oil

4 oz / 100g butter

5 oz / 125g button mushrooms washed and cut in quarters

8 oz / 200g red seedless grapes cut in half

6 oz / 150g dry white wine

STOCK

1 onion

1 carrot

1 stick of celery

all chopped roughly parsley stalks and bay leaf

Cut the breasts from the carcass and trim then reserve in cling film. Put the carcass in a pan with the stock vegetables, cover with 4 pints of cold water bring to the boil and simmer for about 1 hour 30 minutes, strain through a conical strainer and reserve.

Heat the oven 220C/425F/Gas 7 then in a large frying pan add the oil and half the butter, fry the breasts on all sides till lightly browned about 10-12 minutes each [do not over cook or the flesh will become very dry] remove from pan and reserve.

Add the mushrooms to the juices and cook for 3 minutes add the grapes and heat through thoroughly then remove them from the liquor and keep warm.

Drain off the oil from the pan, add the wine and boil for 5 minutes add the $^3/_4$ pint of stock and simmer for about 12 minutes until the sauce begins to thicken strain through a fine sieve into a clean pan.

Warm the pheasant breasts, mushrooms and grapes in the oven for one minute only, meanwhile bring the sauce to the boil and whisk in the rest of the butter to give the sauce a glaze.

Cut the breasts into three slices and arrange on the plates with the mushrooms and grapes pour sauce over and serve.

MARQUISE POTATOES

Prep time: 30 minutes

Cooking time: 20 minutes

2 lb / 900g old potatoes

3 oz / 75g butter

2 eggs

Seasoning

3 tomatoes peeled and pips removed

Wash and cut up the potatoes into chunks, place in a pan, covering with cold water, seasoned with salt.

Bring to the boil, cover with a lid simmer for 25 minutes until cooked. Strain in a colander put back in to the saucepan and put on a gentle heat to get rid of any excess water.

Remove from the heat, mash thoroughly, add the butter, eggs and mix together till a creamy consistency, allow to cool a little before piping.

Grease a baking tray, transfer potatoes to a piping bag with a large star shaped tube. Pipe out nests about $1^1/_2$ inches high and 2 inches wide, pipe out 6 nests and leave to settle for about 10 minutes.

Chop the tomatoes into dice and with a teaspoon place the tomatoes in the centre of the nests of potatoes. Preheat an oven 220C/425F/Gas 7 and place the nests on the top shelf and cook for about 15-20 minutes until the nests are a nice golden brown, remove from oven, allow to stand for about 3 minutes then with a palette knife transfer to a heated serving dish.

BRAISED FENNEL AU GRATIN

Prep time: 10 minutes

Cooking time: 20 minutes

3 Fennel root

$^1/_2$ pint milk

4 oz / 100g grated Cheddar cheese

1 oz / 25g plain flour

$1^1/_2$ oz / 40g butter

Cut the fennel into 4 and remove some of the root base, wash well then place in a pan and cover with the milk, bring to the boil and simmer for 12 minutes.

Remove from the milk and place in a buttered baking dish. Put the butter into a pan and melt add the flour to make a roux, slowly add the milk to make a sauce, season for taste then add to the fennel, top with the cheese, bake in a preheated oven 220C/425F/Gas 7 for 20 minutes or until a nice golden brown.

VICHY CARROTS

Prep time: 5 minutes

Cooking time: 20 minutes

1 lb / 450g firm carrots

2 oz / 50g butter

Chopped fresh parsley

Peel the carrots and cut into slices, place in a pan of cold salted water to just cover the carrots, cover with some buttered greaseproof paper, cut a little hole in the centre for the water to evaporate.

Cook for about 20 minutes until the carrots are just cooked, serve in a vegetable dish, and sprinkle with parsley.

POACHED PEARS SERVED WITH A VANILLA CREAM SAUCE

Prep time: 12 minutes

Cooking time: 20 minutes

6 Comice pears all with stalks

Juice of 1 lemon

1 pint water

4 oz / 100g caster sugar

1 vanilla pod

SAUCE

Prep time: 5 minutes

Cooking time: 10 minutes

4 egg yolks

2 oz / 50g caster sugar

$1/2$ pint full cream milk

Peel the pears and remove the core from the base leaving the stalks intact. Put in a pan, the water, lemon juice, sugar and vanilla pod, bring to the boil. Place 3 pears at a time in the pan and poach for about 15 minutes until cooked but still firm. Remove to a dish and allow cooling, then continue to cook the remaining 3 pears, allowing to cool with the others. Remove vanilla pod and dry.

Put the egg yolks and sugar into a mixer and whisk for about 5 minutes until they are quite pale and stiff. Put the milk and vanilla pod in a pan and heat until nearly boiling, remove the vanilla pod and whisk into the mixture, return to the pan and over a low heat stir with a wooden spoon for about 5 minutes till the mixture thickens, [but do not allow to boil or the sauce will split] if the mixture is getting hot just remove from the heat and keep mixing then return to the heat.

This sauce can be flavoured with a liquor and Grand Marnier is very good.

Serve pear on the centre of a plate pour sauce round the pear and garnish with a mint leaf.

The cold weather is closing in and we are keeping the fire burning with those glowing embers making our evenings look a treat. With the matter of glowing embers we think of Guy Fawkes who tried to blow up the Houses of Parliament so bonfires are this months trait with Bonfire Toffee a must. With regards to food we need to keep our stomachs well fed and warm to keep out those bugs, which are lurking about so hot meals are the in thing. This means a little bit of forethought for our meal, but by now you have grasped a lot of ideas from the book and maybe you are now experimenting with you own ideas.

STILTON, WATERCRESS AND WALNUT TERRINE
WITH SHERRY AND TOMATO CREAM

Prep time: 18 minutes

Cooking time: 30 minutes

8 oz / 200g watercress

8 oz / 200g Stilton

6 oz / 150g Mascarpone cheese

4 oz / 100g strong cheddar cheese

2 eggs

2 tbsp single cream

2 oz / 50g walnuts

4 tsp cream sherry

$1/2$ tsp Dijon mustard

4 tbsp sieved tomatoes

Walnut oil for greasing

Paprika and seasoning

3 small tomatoes

Put the watercress in a large pan of salted water after one minute drain and run under cold water, when cold squeeze out the excess water and form into balls, save some for the tomatoes.

Cut the stilton and cheddar into pieces, put in a processor add two thirds of the mascarpone and blend till smooth, with the motor still running add the eggs, cream and mustard, blend till smooth and scrape into a bowl.

Chop the watercress and halve the walnuts, mix with the cheese mixture and season with black pepper. Take 6 small ramekin moulds, smear with the walnut oil, line the base with greaseproof paper and brush with the oil.

Spoon in the mixture and stand in a roasting tray, half fill with hot water and bake in the oven 200C/400F/Gas 6 for 30 minutes, remove from oven, run a knife around the sides to loosen, turn out on a plate, garnish with half a tomato cut zigzag round the middle, pips removed and filled with some chopped watercress, topped with a walnut.

Beat together the remaining mascarpone, sherry and tomatoes, season with the paprika and salt to taste, serve this sauce separately in a sauce boat or pour round the plate.

RUBANE OF HALIBUT WITH PINK GRAPEFRUIT
AND WHITE WINE SAUCE

Prep time: 25 minutes

Cooking time: 20 minutes

1 lb / 450g halibut, skinned and boned

7 oz / 175g salmon fillet skinned

1 egg white

$^1/_2$ pint double cream

1 tbsp chopped chives

3 leaves of Savoy cabbage

SAUCE

Prep time: 10 minutes

Cooking time: 18 minutes

1 finely chopped onion

4 oz / 100g butter

$^1/_2$ pint double cream

$^1/_4$ pint fish stock

$^1/_4$ pint dry white wine

1 pink grapefruit

2 oz / 50g sugar

1 tbsp brandy

Cut the salmon into small pieces put in a food processor to make into a fine mousse, add the egg white then transfer to a bowl. Place the bowl over crushed ice, slowly add the cream and chives, mix thoroughly and allow to chill in the frigerator for at least 45 minutes.

Place skin and bones from the halibut into a pan and cover with cold water, bring to the boil and simmer for only 20 minutes strain into another pan and reduce to $^1/_4$ of a pint. If you cook the fish stock for over 20 minutes it will become cloudy and bitter.

Blanch the cabbage leaves, refresh and dry.

Butter 6 ramekins and place in a roasting tray, cut the halibut into rings to fit the bottom of the ramekin, add some salmon mousse and a ring of the cabbage leaves, repeat this but finish with the halibut on the top. Cover each ramekin with buttered greaseproof paper, put some warm water in the roasting tin to come half way up the ramekin, cook in an oven 200C/400F/Gas 6 for 15-20 minutes or until set.

Peel off grapefruit zest cut into fine strips blanch in boiling water for 3 minutes refresh in cold water, segment the grapefruit flesh. Put a tablespoon of water in a pan add sugar and stir over a gentle heat for 3 minutes until the sugar starts to caramelise stir in the brandy add the strips of peel.

FOR THE SAUCE
Sweat off the onion in 2 oz of butter for 2-3 minutes without colour add the wine and fish stock. Boil rapidly until the quantity is reduced by half add the caramel juice and cream then reduce further, season for taste whisk in the rest of the butter to give the sauce glaze.

Turn out the ramekin on to the warm plates garnish with the chives, pour the sauce around finish with some segments of grapefruit.

STUFFED LOIN OF PORK WITH A SAGE AND GARLIC CRUST WITH A MADERIA SAUCE

$2\frac{1}{2}$ lb / 1 kilo loin of pork, boned and skin removed

12 fresh dates, stoned

CRUST

Prep time: 15 minutes
Cooking time: 60 minutes

3 cloves garlic crushed

4 oz / 100g fresh white breadcrumbs

4 oz / 100g sage leaves chopped

3 oz / 75g melted butter and seasoning

SAUCE

Prep time: 4 minutes
Cooking time: 12 minutes

1 onion finely chopped

5 oz / 125g butter

6 tbsp Madeira wine

1 pint chicken stock

Cut an incision along one edge of the loin and fill with the stoned dates, tie with string to keep the dates secure.

Mix all the crust ingredients together and press thickly over the pork, if it does not stick add a little more butter to the mixture.

Place the pork in a roasting tray and cook in the oven 190C/375F/Gas 5 for 45-55 minutes until the joint is cooked.

Put 1 oz butter in a pan, fry off the onions add the wine and stock reduce by half.

Remove the pork from the roasting tray and keep warm, remove the excess fat from the roasting tray and reduce the residue by half, add the sauce and bring to the boil season and strain. (This can be thickened with a gravy mix if required)

Add the rest of the butter to give a glaze.

STIR FRIED SPROUTS WITH PINENUTS

Prep time: 6 minutes
Cooking time: 10 minutes

1¹/₂ lb / 600g Brussels sprouts very thinly sliced

1 oz / 25g pine nuts

2 tbsp boiling water

2 tbsp oil

2 oz / 50g melted butter

Heat a dry wok, add the pine nuts and toast, gently shaking the pan until evenly browned then remove. Add the oil and fry the sprouts for 2-3 minutes add the water and cook for about 4 minutes, season, add the pine nuts and finish with the butter to give a nice glaze, serve immediately.

FONDANTE POTATOES

Prep time: 15 minutes
Cooking time: 25 minutes

1¹/₂ lb / 600g potatoes

4 oz / 100g melted butter

¹/₂ pint chicken stock

Chopped parsley

Try and get your potatoes all the same size about 2 inches long and about 1-1/2 inches wide. Peel each potato to get an oblong shape then hold the potato with your index finger and thumb and trim round the sharp edges to try and make a barrel shape. Stand the potatoes up in an ovenproof dish and pour round the boiling stock to come up halfway on the potatoes, brush over with melted butter season, then place in a preheated oven 220C/425F/Gas 7, cook for about 20-25 minutes until cooked the tops are a nice golden brown and the bases are moist from the stock.

Serve in a vegetable dish, sprinkle with the chopped parsley.

PARSNIP GRATIN WITH HORSERADISH CREAM

Prep time: 5 minutes

Cooking time: 25 minutes

1¹/₂ lb / 600g parsnips

2 oz / 50g butter

1 tbsp horseradish sauce

4 oz / 100g grated strong cheddar cheese

¹/₄ pint single cream

1 oz / 25g chopped parsley

Peel and cut the parsnips into 2 inch wedges across then cut in half and slice thinly.

Cook in boiling salted water for about 5 minutes until just softened.

Strain and toss in the butter, put them in an ovenproof dish, mix the cream and horseradish together with the parsley and pour over the parsnips, sprinkle with the cheese, cook in an oven 200C/400F/Gas 6 for 15-20 minutes until a nice golden brown and serve hot.

ARMAGNAC PARFAIT IN A BRANDY SNAP BASKET
WITH ORANGES AND EARL GREY SYRUP

Prep time: 10 minutes

Cooking time: 8 minutes

BRANDY SNAP BASKET

2 oz / 50g butter

4 oz / 100g castor sugar

4 oz / 100g golden sugar

2 oz / 50g plain flour

1 tsp ground ginger

1 pint stock syrup

2 lb / 800g granulated sugar

18 fl oz water

Prep time: 10 minutes

Cooking time: 20 minutes

6 egg yolks

3 oz / 75g castor sugar

3 tbsp water

$1/_2$ pint double cream

$2^1/_2$ fl oz Armagnac

1 tsp fresh lemon juice

6 earl grey teabags

2 oz / 50g chopped walnuts

2 oranges segmented

In a small pan melt the butter, sugar and syrup over a low heat until the sugar dissolves.

Remove from the heat and beat in the rest of the ingredients. To make, roll 1 oz of paste in a smooth ball, place on parchment paper only 2 on a tray and bake in an oven gas mark 4 for 6-8 minutes until golden brown.

Remove and leave to cool for 30 seconds then using a palette knife drape over a greased mould, leave to set for 3 minutes then remove and allow to set. Use the rest of the mixture to make up 6 baskets.

Note: This mixture can be made well in advance and left in the fridge till needed to be cooked.

Put the sugar and water in a pan, bring to the boil, simmer for 5 minutes, strain through a muslin, leave to cool.

Put a third of the stock syrup in a pan bring to the boil, add the tea bags and allow to infuse for about 6 minutes then remove teabags, add lemon juice and half the Armagnac store in a fridge, this should be like a syrup, if not simmer for a little longer.

Whisk the egg yolks in a mixer until very pale and well risen in volume and stands its own weight [ribbon stage]. Boil the water and castor sugar together until the syrup gets to reach a softball stage [coat a cold spoon with the liquid, then dip the spoon into cold water to set. Pinch a little between your finger and thumb and when it rolls into a soft ball it is ready] this takes about 5 minutes.

Take the pan off the stove, put the base into cold water to stop the cooking, wipe the base of the pan and pour into the egg yolks with the whisk running, reduce the speed and whisk for 5 minutes.

In another bowl whisk the cream and the rest of the Armagnac until it just starts to thicken, mix in the walnuts. Fold the cream into the yolks and sugar mixture, pour into 6 dariole moulds, cover and freeze. Place one basket on each plate in the centre arrange 2 orange segments on each plate on the outside pour a little syrup, turn out the parfaits in the baskets [if they do not come out easily, dip in hot water for a few seconds run the tip of a knife round the top and invert].

Drizzle a little syrup over the parfaits and serve.

55

Well Christmas is nearly here and most of us get invited to parties both at homes and staff parties at work and when you go to the staff party what is on the menu, we all know it is turkey, so by the end of December we are quite sick of it, though very nice on the day. Another factor with this month is the amount of food we consume when eating Christmas cake and mince pies all we want to do is sleep or have a nap in the afternoon, at least that is what I sometimes do. When friends or family visit you for a meal I have tried to make it fairly simple and not too filling so you can sit down with them.

RED PEPPER AND COURGETTE MOUSSE WITH A LIME AND PARSLEY HOLLANDAISE

Prep time: 20 minutes

Cooking time: 40 minutes

3 red peppers

1 courgette thinly sliced

1 courgette diced

Chopped fresh parsley

3 eggs

1 oz / 25g Parmesan cheese

2 fl oz single cream

2 tbsp olive oil

1 x 1/2 Pint packet of hollandaise mix

Juice of 1 lime

3 tomatoes and cucumber for garnish

Cut the peppers in half, remove the seeds, place on a baking sheet and cook under a grill for about 15 minutes until the skins are charred and blistered all over.

Place in a plastic bag, seal and leave to cool. Remove the skins, place peppers and diced courgette in a food processor and cream for one minute, add the eggs, cream, cheese, and parsley and season, cream for about 2 minutes.

Heat the oil in a frying pan, fry the sliced courgette for about 6 minutes until tender, remove and dry on kitchen paper. Grease 6 ramekin dishes, put some of the pepper mixture in the bottom put some of the sliced courgettes in then again some more of the mixture then some courgette, finish with the pepper mixture.

Place the ramekin in a roasting dish, pour hot water half way up the ramekin to make a Bain Marie place them in a preheated oven 200C/400F/Gas 6 and cook for about 30 minutes.

Remove from roasting tin and allow to cool, then placing in a fridge till ready to serve.

Mix up the hollandaise as per instructions, mix in the lime juice and chopped parsley.

Turn out the mousse on a plate and drizzle round some of the hollandaise garnish with tomato rose and cucumber.

Top Tip
These can be made well in advance

MELON COCKTAIL WITH PRAWNS

Prep time: 20 minutes

3 ripe Ogen melons

1 ripe Charentais melon

8 oz / 225g large prawns

1 jar cocktail sauce

With a small sharp knife cut a zigzag round the middle of the Ogen melons to form six bases for your cocktail. Scoop out the pips, then with a melon baller scoop out the centres into a bowl.

Cut the other melon in half and remove the pips. Scoop out with a melon baller into the bowl with the other melon.

Mix together thoroughly so you have two colours evenly distributed. With a sharp knife cut a very little off the bottom of each base so it does not roll about and has a base to sit perfectly on a plate.

Wash the prawns well, add to your melons, mix together and distribute to the six halves of melon, leave in fridge till needed.

To serve put on a plate with a doily underneath, put the cocktail sauce over and if you have some prawns left over put round the melon top for a garnish.

TOMATO AND HERB CRUSTED FILLED OF BEEF

Prep time: 10 minutes

Cooking time: 45 minutes

2 lb / 800g thick end fillet of beef

1 tbsp olive oil

1 egg

2 tbsp whole grain mustard

5 tbsp sun-dried tomato paste

5 tbsp dried breadcrumbs

1 x 400g chopped tomatoes well drained

1 tbsp chopped fresh parsley

2 tsp chopped fresh rosemary

2 tsp chopped fresh thyme

2 whole peeled shallots

SAUCE

Prep time: 4 minutes

Cooking time: 25 minutes

1 oz / 25g butter

1 finely chopped onion

2 tbsp cranberry jelly

6 fl oz beef stock

8 fl oz red wine

3 tbsp port

1 tsp wholegrain mustard

2 tsp cornflour

Put a long strip of cling film on a board place the fillet in the middle then roll up into a sausage fashion and with the overhang at each end, roll together to form a very tight fit, put in fridge to relax for 12 hours.

Remove the cling film from the meat and tie into a neat shape round the middle at intervals, using a fine string. Heat half the oil in a frying pan seal the meat all over until evenly browned. Allow to cool then remove the strings.

Place the meat in a roasting tin, spread evenly with the mustard. Mix together the tomato paste, breadcrumbs, herbs and one tablespoon of olive oil and season. Press evenly over the top of the beef.

Place around the beef the shallots, and to the roasting tray the rest of the oil. Roast in a preheated oven 220C/425F/Gas 7 for 20 minutes for rare or 30 minutes for medium.

Remove from tray cover with tinfoil and allow resting for 8 minutes. Strain off any residue from the meat save the shallots and remove any fat from the residue.

SAUCE
Melt the butter in a pan add the onions and cook for 5 minutes do not allow to colour add the rest of the ingredients, bring to the boil and simmer for 10 minutes. Add the residue and continue to simmer for a further 6 minutes, thicken with the cornflour, taste for flavour and season if necessary.

Carve the meat onto the plates add two shallots to each plate and pour a little of the sauce round the plate, garnish with watercress.

SPICED CREAMY POTATOES

Prep time: 8 minutes

Cooking time: 20 minutes

1 lb / 450g potatoes

1 oz / 25g butter

$^1/_2$ tsp ground coriander

$^1/_2$ tsp grated nutmeg

Chopped parsley

2 tbsp single cream

Peel the potatoes and cook for 20 minutes or until done, strain in a colander, return to saucepan and mash.

Add the butter, cream and season to taste, finally add the coriander, nutmeg and parsley and beat well.

Serve in a heated vegetable dish.

FANTAIL LEMON GARLIC POTATOES

Prep time: 12 minutes

Cooking time: 40 minutes

12 small even-sized potatoes

2 cloves garlic

Juice of 2 fresh lemons

2 oz / 50g butter

1 oz / 25g lard

Peel the potatoes and put a skewer through about 2 thirds of the potato and with a sharp knife cut down to the skewer in slices making sure not to cut right through, rinse in cold water and pat dry with kitchen paper.

Put the butter and lard in a roasting tray add the garlic and lemon juice and allow to simmer together for 2 minutes, add the potatoes and roll in the mixture until fully covered place in a preheated oven 200C/400F/Gas 6 for about 35-40 minutes or until cooked and a golden brown, serve in a hot vegetable dish.

BUTTERED LEEKS WITH TARRAGON

Prep time: 10 minutes

Cooking time: 12 minutes

1 lb / 400g leeks washed and trimmed

3 oz / 75g butter

1 large bunch of tarragon

Cut the leeks into 3-inch lengths, then cut into 4 length ways and wash well.

Drain and pat dry with kitchen paper. Melt the butter in a pan add the leeks, tie the tarragon into a bunch using strong string with an overlap and place in the pan with the leeks, put a lid on top and simmer slowly over a low heat for about 10 minutes or until the leeks are tender.

Remove the tarragon and toss the leeks together season for taste and serve hot in a dish.

BUTTERED SPROUTS WITH ALMONDS

Prep time: 8 minutes

Cooking time: 14 minutes

1$^{1}/_{2}$ lb / 600g small sprouts

2 oz / 50g butter

4 oz / 100g flake almonds

2 oz / 50g sugar

Peel the sprouts and wash well in salted water strain in a colander.

Cook the sprouts in boiling salted water but just before putting the sprouts in add the sugar this will keep them green.

Cook for about 10 minutes until just firm, drain and set aside.

Melt the butter in a large frying pan add the sprouts and almonds toss together until the almonds are evenly distributed season to taste and serve at once.

CHOCOLATE MERINGUE LOG

Prep time: 12 minutes

Cooking time: 45 minutes

1 tsp cornflour

1 tsp vinegar

1 tsp vanilla essence

4 egg whites

8 oz / 225g castor sugar

2 oz / 50g grated dark chocolate

FILLING

Prep time: 12 minutes

2 oz / 50g milk chocolate

7 fl oz whipping cream

1 tbsp rum or brandy

HOLLY LEAVES

Prep time: 15 minutes

2 oz / 50g dark chocolate

2 oz / 50g white chocolate

Preheat the oven 160C/300F/Gas 2 and line a Swiss roll tin 9 x 13 x $^3/_4$ in with greaseproof paper.

Blend the cornflour, essence and vinegar together. Whisk the egg whites in a mixer till stiff, whisk in the sugar and a tablespoon of the corn flour mixture in between till all has been used and the mixture is stiff and a marshmallow consistency. Fold in the grated chocolate, spoon into the Swiss roll tin and spread over the base till evenly distributed. Bake in a preheated oven 160C/300F/Gas 2 for 45 minutes, remove and cover with foil until cool, about 15 minutes.

Make the filling, melt the chocolate in a bowl over a pan of hot water [not boiling], remove and allow to cool. Beat the cream and rum or brandy until thickened, fold into the chocolate when cool with a large metal spoon.

Turn the meringue onto a sheet of greaseproof paper, peel off the lining paper, trim the edges to make it easier to roll. Spread some of the filling over the meringue [saving a spoon full for later] carefully roll up the meringue using the greaseproof as a guide, transfer to a serving platter and chill for one hour.

HOLLY LEAVES
Draw holly leaves on greaseproof paper. Heat the dark and white chocolate separately in bowls set over hot, but not boiling water and stir till melted.

Spoon into separate greaseproof paper bags cut a small piece off the base of each bag and with the dark chocolate pipe round the outside of each holly leaf, then with the white flood the middle of the leaf.

While the chocolate is still soft pipe a line of dark chocolate down the middle and with a cocktail stick, feather the dark chocolate out to form the veins of the holly do this at intervals.

When meringue is cold remove from the greaseproof, with the reserved filling secure chocolate leaves to the top of the meringue the log can be kept in a fridge for up to two hours before serving. This can be served with fresh cream if desired.

HANDY HINTS & TIPS

Making a White Sauce

Melt the butter in a small saucepan over a low heat blend in the flour and cook over a low heat for 1-2 minutes, stirring constantly with a wooden spoon until the mixture resembles a soft marzipan.

Remove the pan from the heat and gradually add the milk. Mixing well until smooth. Return to the pan to a low heat and bring to the boil, stirring all the time with a wooden spoon. Cook for 2-3 minutes, stirring constantly until the sauce is thickened and smooth and the flour is properly cooked.

Making Filo Boats

To cut out oval shapes for the boat-shaped moulds, use greaseproof paper to make a template 1/2 inch larger all round that the top of the moulds. Keep the unused filo pastry covered with a damp clothe to stop it drying out. Brush each layer of filo with melted butter during shaping to keep it pliable. Press the buttered pastry firmly into each mould to make them fairly strong. Trim with scissors.

Skinning Peppers

Cut the pepper in half length ways and, skin-sides up, cook under a hot grill until the skin blisters (about 3-4 minutes). Place the charred peppers in a plastic bag for about 5 minutes and allow to sweat. The skin can then be scraped away with a knife. Rinse thoroughly. If you have an oven on you can put them in until they are black and the put in a plastic bag.

Clarifying Butter

Melt the butter in a pan, remove from the heat and leave to stand so the sediment settles to the base. Slowly pour through a sieve lined with muslin to strain out salty particles which may catch and burn during cooking.

Segmenting Grapefruit and Oranges

Cut a thin slice of peel from the top and bottom of the fruit so it stands up on either end, place one end on your board. Cut barrel fashion round the peel to remove all the pith. Hold the fruit over a bowl to catch any juice and cut into each segment with a sharp knife, cutting inside the thin membrane on both sides of each segment to loosen the fruit.

Coating a souffle Dish

Always prepare the dish before you begin to make the souffle, because once you have whisked the mixture you will have to work quickly to prevent it from sticking. Grease the dish with melted butter, then dust with caster sugar, this coating helps give the mixture a grip as it cooks.

Making Chocolate Leaves

Put some chocolate in a bowl and heat over a pan of simmering water stirring all the time.

Make sure you wash and dry the rose leaves before use to remove any chemicals from garden sprays. Brush a layer of melted chocolate over the back of rose leaves and leave to set. Carefully peel off the chocolate from the rose leaves and store in the refrigerator.

Herbs & Spices

ALLSPICE

These berries are the small round, aromatic evergreen of the myrtle and clove family, which can grow to over 40 feet. Picked when green and unripe, they are dried in the sun to a rich, deep brown colour, they are similar in shape and size to a peppercorn, but less wrinkled. Native to the West Indies, allspice grows prolifically in Jamaica where it is widely used in native dishes. Its flavour, the likes of cloves, cinnamon, and nut-meg with cloves predominating, gives allspice its name.

It is used a lot by the Swedish in their smorgasbord and in savoury dishes, smoked and pickled foods such as raw fish, salami and other Continental sausages. As a sweet spice it is used ground in pies, cakes and puddings, especially in Christmas pudding recipes.

ANISEED

A native of the Middle East, the aromatic anise annual grows to about 2 feet high, and the small, oval, grey-green ribbed seeds should be bought whole in small quantities and stored in the dark.

Its spicy/sweet flavour combines well with both sweet and savoury foods. It is used in northern and Eastern Europe in confectionery, desserts, biscuits, cakes and bread. It is a favourite seasoning in Indian fish curries and marinades. The seeds are often dry roasted in a frying pan to extract their full flavour.

CARDAMOM

This bush is a relative of the ginger plant and grows nearly 10 feet high, its pod-bearing stalks sprawling along the ground. Native to these Countries: India, China, Latin America and parts of Indonesia.

The aroma is unique and unmistakable, its flavour is sweet but clean with a hint of eucalyptus, it is an expensive spice. Green cardamom is widely available, and the black variety can be acquired from Indian grocers. Buy the pods whole and crush them to release the seeds if these are needed separately, but remember that the pods themselves cannot be eaten. Store pods in an airtight container.

USES. Is one of the essential spices in Indian food and curries and also imparts its flavour to many Indian sweet dishes and beverages.

CARAWAY

Caraway has been found in the remains of Stone Age meals, Egyptian tombs and ancient caravan stops along the Orient Silk Road. Roman soldiers ate the roots mixed with milk and made4 it into bread. It is found in all parts of Europe. It is a hardy biennial 8 inches in the first year, 2ft high in the second year. Finely cut leaves, white flowers in June.

USES. Sprinkle seeds over pork, goose and rich stews to aid digestion. Gives flavour to soups, breads, cakes, biscuits and apple pies. Add seeds to cabbage water to reduce cooking smells. Bake with fruit and chop leaves into salads.

CHERVIL

Chervil is a culinary herb that has been used since Roman times. It has a special delicate parsley-like taste with a hint of aniseed and is used extensively in the French cuisine. It is one of the first herbs to be found after the winter season.

USES. It is used fresh at the end of cooking in great quantities to appreciate its flavour. Try substituting it for parsley. Leaves can be used in salads, soups, sauces, chicken, egg dishes and fruit cocktails.

CORIANDER

USES. The leaves and seeds have two distinct flavours. Seeds are normally aromatic, whereas the leaves have an earthy pungent taste. Use seeds in chutneys, curries, apple pies, cakes, stir fries and biscuits. Add to soups, sauces and vegetable dishes. Seeds are sometimes used to flavour gin. Add fresh leaves to curries, stews, salads, sauces and use as a garnish.

CHILLI

Chilli peppers are very fiery and a very ancient spice and originate in Latin America they belong to the capsicum branch of the plant family. Many different types of fresh and dried chillies are easily acquired; one can choose between fresh unripe or ripe whole chillies, dried whole chillies, chilli powders, and chilli seasonings. For the unaccustomed it is better to be cautious when preparing chillies and wear gloves during preparation. Never touch your eyes or mouth when you are preparing these, as they are very pungent.

USES. The best dish for its use is chilli con carne that is made all over the world and you must realise that it is used to add a fiery flavour to many dishes and must be used very carefully.

Herbs & Spices

CINNAMON

It grows in many tropical areas, including its native Sri Lanka, southern India, Brazil and the West Indies. The tropical cinnamon evergreen can reach a height of 30feet or more, but it is from its young cultivated shoots that the bark is harvested. The dried bark is sold as a spice in small quills usually 3-6 inches long, or as a powder.

USES. It is a very popular spice used in savoury dishes such as to flavour meat or vegetables such as aubergines and courgettes. Many European cakes and puddings, especially those dishes using apple include it in there dishes.

DILL

The dill plant is a member of the parsley family and the leaves and stalks can be used in cooking. They have a fresh, sweet aroma but a slightly bitter taste, somewhat similar to caraway seeds.

USES. The seeds are good in pickled dishes, vinegars, marinades and dressings. It is also used in chicken and vegetable dishes, it is used in sauerkraut. fish, sole, plaice, haddock and mackerel. It can be used in batters, marinades and spiced breadcrumbs for either fish or poultry.

FENNEL SEEDS

Fennel is best known in Europe, especially around the Mediterranean, as a herb, salad ingredient and vegetable, but its dried seeds are also valuable in cooking. Like dill and anise, fennel is a member of the parsley family.

USES. Fennel seeds are universally used with fish as they give that extra flavour to all kinds of fish, sole, plaice, haddock and mackerel. It can be used in batters, marinades and spiced breadcrumbs for either fish or poultry.

GINGER

Ginger is an important spice both in the East and West. Like other tropical plants of the same family, such as the galangals and turmeric, it is the knobbly root of the ginger plant that is used as a culinary spice. Fresh ginger root, essential for the exotic cuisines of many Eastern lands, it is peeled, then sliced, chopped, grated or ground to a paste and used to flavour dishes of fish, chicken and meat. The tenderest parts of the rhizomes near the stem are preserved in syrup and sold as stem ginger. You will find that ground ginger is used in baking and is sold in many Supermarkets.

HORSERADISH

A hardy perennial with wavy, indented leaves and tiny white flowers, horseradish grows 2-3 feet high and has a thick, buff coloured taproot. The root is grated and is very strong like onions; it is mixed with cream and served as a compliment for roast beef. It can be combined with mustard in a sauce for fish, chicken, eggs or vegetables, or in stewed apples in a sauce for duck or goose.

LEMON BALM

It is a perennial growing to about 3 feet with aromatic leaves, which give off a strong lemon fragrance when crushed. It produces small pinkish-white flowers during mid summer. The leaves can be chopped and added to stuffing's for poultry and game, salads deserts and fruit cups.

LEMON GRASS

It is a perennial and a native to South-East Asia. It has pointed aromatic leaves, sharp and spiky, with a slightly swollen leaf base. Lemon grass is easy to grow in pots if you can manage to get hold of a root.
The lower sections of the leaves contain aromatic oil, which is strong in lemon flavour. It is used in curries and spiced dishes, but is very good to flavour fish dishes and can be removed when the dish is cooked as it has a wonderful lemon flavour.

MINT

As we all know mint is very much used in this country and there are several types that are grown here ex apple, pineapple, spearmint and black peppermint plus a lot more. If you grow mint always put it in a large bucket in your garden or it could take over your vegetable bed very soon. Mint is very good in flavouring new potatoes, peas and several vegetables but foremost it is a compliment to roast lamb.

PARSLEY

A hardy biennial growing from 6-8 inches high. Parsley first grew in south Eastern Europe, near the Mediterranean and was probably bought to Briton by the Romans.
USES in the UK parsley is used mainly as a garnish, but with its delicious flavour it ca be used widely in cooking for stuffing's, marinades, mixed with bread crumbs and fried to put over cooked cauliflower. To make a fresh parsley sauce, to cook with fish to add that extra flavour, parsley is something that should always be in a kitchen as it has so much use.

ROSEMARY

It is a bushy shrub, often growing over 4 feet high. It is a perennial but being delicate, it sometimes fails to survive a hard winter. It has evergreen needles, dark green on top and silvery grey underneath. It produces light blue flowers in early summer, which attract bees, and is a native of eastern Mediterranean.
Indeed its flavour is so robust it can be overpowering, and should be used in strict moderation. Sprigs of the herb must be removed from the dish after cooking, as the needles remain hard and sharp and can be dangerous. Rosemary is best used to flavour roast mutton and lamb, or in stuffing's for strongly flavoured meat and game.